"Gordon Smith ke
clarity and breatht:
covers ground we t
us things we misse

Mark Buchanan, author of *Your Church Is Too Safe*

"In *Teach Us to Pray*, Gordon Smith teaches about prayer in a way that digs much deeper into Christian formation than simply discussing prayer as a spiritual practice. Straightforward, but never simplistic, this little book challenges us to see prayer as rooted in a comprehensive vision of Christianity actively lived in the kingdom of God. Grounded in the goodness and love of God, prayer calls us to a life of gratitude, penitence, and discernment, all led by the Holy Spirit, all combining to bring us into genuine spiritual transformation. What Smith teaches about prayer is not easy or automatic, but if you want to understand prayer as Jesus lived it out, if you want to be discipled in prayer, *Teach Us to Pray* offers that hope."

Steve Breedlove, bishop, Diocese of Christ our Hope, Anglican Church in North America

TEACH US TO PRAY

GORDON T. SMITH

IVP Books

An imprint of InterVarsity Press
Downers Grove, Illinois

InterVarsity Press
P.O. Box 1400, Downers Grove, IL 60515-1426
ivpress.com
email@ivpress.com

*InterVarsity Press® is the book-publishing division of InterVarsity Christian Fellowship/USA®,
a movement of students and faculty active on campus at hundreds of universities, colleges, and
schools of nursing in the United States of America, and a member movement of the International
Fellowship of Evangelical Students. For information about local and regional activities,
visit intervarsity.org.*

*Scripture quotations, unless otherwise noted, are from the New Revised Standard Version of the
Bible, copyright 1989 by the Division of Christian Education of the National Council of the
Churches of Christ in the USA. Used by permission. All rights reserved.*

*While any stories in this book are true, some names and identifying information may have been
changed to protect the privacy of individuals.*

Cover design: David Fassett
Interior design: Daniel van Loon

ISBN 978-0-8308-4521-7 (print)
ISBN 978-0-8308-8846-7 (digital)

Printed in the United States of America ∞

Library of Congress Cataloging-in-Publication Data
A catalog record for this book is available from the Library of Congress.

P 25 24 23 22 21 20 19 18 17 16 15 14 13 12 11 10 9 8 7 6 5 4 3 2 1

Y 37 36 35 34 33 32 31 30 29 28 27 26 25 24 23 22 21 20 19 18

to joella

CONTENTS

PREFACE

Practicing Prayer

*i*t is a poignant encounter that the disciples have with Jesus, a tender moment, when they see Jesus returning from being in prayer and say to him, "Lord, teach us to pray" (Luke 11:1). I am inclined to quote their request with an intentional emphasis on the word *us*. Teach *us* to pray. They longed to enter into a practice that was clearly vital to the life and ministry of Jesus. They too wanted to pray.

This request is a reminder to us that one of the most basic capacities of the Christian—a basic spiritual discipline—is the practice of prayer. The Scriptures assume that prayer is a vital dimension or element of the Christian life—for the Christian and for the church. The Christian spiritual tradition assumes that the church is a praying community; to be a Christian is to be a pray-er. It can truly be said that we cannot live the Christian life unless we learn how to pray. We cannot be the church until we pray.

And thus it is important to give time and focus to the meaning and practice of prayer, given its central place in our lives and the life of the church. It is important to learn *how* to pray. It follows, then, that it is important to be part of a Christian community, a church, that teaches prayer. It is a basic spiritual practice. So it only makes sense that the essential work of Christian catechesis—the ministry of introducing new Christians to the faith—includes teaching on how to pray. As for older, more mature Christians, we need to come back to the basics, the fundamentals of prayer, in that we are always learning how to pray. The church only lives as it prays; Christians only grow in faith, hope, and love as they learn how to pray.

This book offers a reminder that as the church, as Christians in community, we long to learn together what it means to pray. But while I consider the church at prayer, the focus in what follows is on how each of us, individually and personally, can and needs to know how to pray—even as Jesus prayed. We learn to pray in community as part of the church, and we learn to pray alone in solitude. Our personal prayers lean into and draw on the experience of the church at prayer. But my focus will be on our personal and individual prayers as we ask what it means to learn how to pray.

PRAYER AND THE
KINGDOM OF GOD

*i*n learning how to pray, it is, of course, helpful to go to the very prayer that Jesus gave his disciples when they asked, "Teach *us* to pray." He taught them to say what we know as the Lord's Prayer, or in some Christian communities, the Our Father. The prayer is a sequence of prayers: "hallowed be thy name," "forgive us our debts," and "give us this day." Yet these prayers pivot on one prayer or petition in particular: "thy kingdom come," and its twin, "thy will be done in earth, as it is in heaven" (Matthew 6:9-11 KJV). Essentially, then, Jesus taught his disciples to pray for the coming of the kingdom—for coming of the reign of God. When we pray "thy kingdom come," we are expressing the longing of our hearts and minds that the will of God would happen, on earth as it is in heaven.

It would be a profound understatement to say that this matters. For indeed nothing matters more. Nothing. The idea of the kingdom of God permeates the whole of the witness of the Old Testament; we read again and again of the longing for the future manifestation of the reign of God. From this vantage point, the prayer is a longing, in the Jewish tradition, for the coming of the Messiah. Jesus himself spoke of how he would not drink of the fruit of the vine again "until the kingdom of God comes" (Luke 22:18). And this is the prayer of the church: for the coming of the kingdom, for Christ to return and bring about the restoration and healing of the entire created order. We yearn for the consummation of the reign of Christ: that Christ—the Messiah—would be revealed, and that all creation would know the full manifestation of the healing and restorative grace of God.

Theologians therefore speak of this as an *eschatological* prayer—looking ahead to a day that is yet to come. That day is when the purposes of God—now very present in heaven, where God dwells—will be fully consummated on earth, where we dwell. Our great longing and prayer, in other words, is not to "go to heaven" but for heaven to come down and transform the earth and all its inhabitants and thus reveal the glory and purposes of God (see Revelation 21).

And yet when Jesus—the very one who announced that the kingdom of God is at hand (Mark 1:14-15)—offers this prayer, we have to also read it through another lens. Yes, the kingdom is future; we look forward to a day that is yet to come; we anticipate the consummation of the kingdom. But the kingdom of God is also very present. The disciples of

Jesus are those who now live in him and under his authority. We have become and are becoming citizens of this kingdom, living now, in the present, in and under the reign of Christ. His disciples are those who seek his kingdom and even now, as a foretaste of what is yet to come, begin to allow the will of God—"thy will be done in earth, as it is in heaven"—to be effective and expressed in every sphere and dimension of human life—indeed, of the whole cosmos. This begins in particular, of course, in our own lives. In our prayers, we learn obedience; very specifically, we learn the freedom that comes in and through obedience within the benevolent reign of Christ. In our prayers we enter into the grace of deferring to the will and authority of Christ.

This is our great longing: to enter into his kingdom. Jesus suggests that we should seek the kingdom, that this is the most important agenda in our lives. It is worth any price; it merits the full scope of our energies and desires. We are invited not only to pray the prayer but also, in praying, to enter *into* the kingdom—to seek it and to live in this new dimension of reality. Saint Paul urges us to set our minds on things that are above (Colossians 3:2), which means precisely the same thing—to live with our minds set on Christ, who is the ascended Lord and whose reign has come and is coming.

As an aside, though an important consideration: all of this is a reminder that the gospel *necessarily* includes the reality that Christ is the ascended Lord. For too many Christians the gospel speaks merely of the cross of Christ and the forgiveness that is found in and through the cross. This is gospel, of course, but is it the whole of the gospel? Surely the proclamation of the gospel also presumes the declaration that Jesus Christ is Lord and that, in the words of Jesus, "the kingdom of God has come near" (Mark 1:15). When we yearn for the salvation of God, we long for women and men to know forgiveness—of course. But we also long that the kingdom of God would come, that God's will would be done on earth. That is, in the language of Philippians 2:10-11, we look forward to the day when every knee will bow and every tongue confess that Jesus Christ is Lord. And what that means is the healing and restoration of the creation and the triumph of justice, so that all things come under the benevolent authority of Christ.

PRAYER AND PARTICIPATION

When Jesus teaches his disciples to pray he invites them to seek the kingdom and to pray that the will of God, the reign of Christ, would be expressed in every sphere of their lives. This is our prayer. This is the deep longing, the yearning of the human soul and of all of humanity: we pray that all would be restored, redeemed, and healed. But it also makes full sense that we would pray this not only in a general sense but also with regard to the specifics of our lives. We truly pray this prayer only when our praying actually draws us into the reign of Christ—that is, into the very thing for which we are praying. The prayer is not passive but active; it is a prayer that *alters* our lives. We pray "thy kingdom come" even as we seek the kingdom and long to enter more fully into Christ and allow the reign of Christ to inform and transform our lives.

We pray "thy kingdom come" in the particulars of our individual lives—our families, our workplaces, our neighborhoods. And we pray it for our cities, our country, and our world. We pray it for the church. And we long for God to act—mercifully and graciously. Our very praying reflects a confidence that God will act. But even as we pray, in our praying, we are changed. Our prayer is answered very specifically in our own lives as God grants us the grace of living in the kingdom. In other words, it is surely fine to pray for specific things: *I need a job, a home for my family, healing for a loved one*—indeed, all the things for which we might pray. But while prayer for what we need and what we long for is without doubt appropriate, we must remember that there is more to prayer than petition. In our praying not only are we asking God to change things, but we are being changed. More specifically, if and as we learn to pray, we become women and men who live in and under the reign of Christ.

So easily prayer becomes little more than asking God to act, asking God to do what only God can do, asking God to intervene and through mercy bring about God's purposes in the particulars of our lives. But we are not mere observers of what God is doing in bringing about the kingdom. We are participants. Or as Darrell Johnson puts it, in this prayer we "participate in heaven's invasion of the earth" and thus experience more and more what it means to see and live within the reign of Christ, here on earth.

I serve as the president of a university that, like most of our peer institutions, has a dynamic and exciting athletic program. When our volleyball team is on the court facing a visiting team, especially from a school with which we have a bit of a rivalry, it can be quite intense—not only on the court but also in the stands. And of course I cheer eagerly for the young women and men who wear our university colors with a hope to win a championship and have a banner hung from the rafters. I always like it when we win, of course; and I particularly like it when we beat the sister institution with which we have a focused and historic rivalry.

But imagine that we are losing—it is a very close game, but we are losing. In moments like that we wonder what small but significant factor could change the outcome. I notice that the coach calls a time-out; surely he recognizes that he needs to make a strategic adjustment so that this close game shifts in our favor. But imagine that I do not wait patiently through the time-out, but rather conclude that as the president of the university I need to do my part. So I leave the stands, head to the huddle on the side of the court, and interrupt the time-out to advise the coach that I am available and willing to do my part. What's more, I think my contribution could make a difference—perhaps the difference that will let us ultimately win the match. I urge him to put me into the game.

Well, of course the coach will patiently ask the president to return to the stands and will assure me that at this point I am only an observer, not a participant! I can only serve well by not getting in the way. I need to head back to the stands.

But it is not so with the kingdom of God. When we pray "thy kingdom come" we are not mere observers in the stands, watching God do God's work and, so to speak, cheering God on. Rather, what is clear from the Scriptures is that while we *are* observers, we not *only* observers. We are also participants.

We are players in the work of God in our world; we are actors on the stage. We are not lead actors; we are not the ones who ultimately make it happen. But we are on the stage; we are players in the drama of God's redemptive purposes in the world. Our lives and our work matter and make a difference.

And so we need an approach to prayer that reflects this reality: that in our prayers we are not only saying the words "thy kingdom come" but also actually entering into the kingdom, knowing—without doubt in small incremental steps, but still knowing more and more—what it means to live in the grace of the kingdom, the freedom that comes in living under the reign of Christ.

PRAYER AS FORMATION

Prayer has a formative impact on our lives—the manner or form of our prayers actually shapes the contours and character of our lives. So frequently, it would seem, our prayers begin with our experience: something in our lives occasions a particular prayer, typically a petition or request. And thus the content of our prayers is determined by what is happening in our lives.

But perhaps the reverse should actually be the norm. Without doubt, the circumstances of our lives will inform our prayers. But perhaps what should be happening is that our prayers would inform our lives, that our praying would alter our living, that our prayers would shape the contours and content of our daily experience.

In this way of living and praying, we would allow our deepest convictions—our faith and our theological vision of God, ourselves, and our world—to inform our prayers and be the *means* by which we know the transforming power of grace in our lives. More particularly, we would choose that the reign of Christ—the kingdom of God—would increasingly be that which defines our lives, our ways of being, living, and responding to our world. We would find that the salvation of God is not merely something that God has done *for* us—in Christ, on the cross—but also something that God is doing *in* us.

To this end, our prayers play a crucial role. Indeed, if transformation does not happen through our prayers, it likely does not happen. This is why it is so crucial that we teach new Christians how to pray and that in our patterns and approaches to congregational life we are consistently coming back to the fundamentals of prayer. And this is why all of us, older and newer Christians alike, are always coming back to the basics of the form and structure of formative prayer.

When we pray "thy kingdom come," should not our prayer be an act of recalibration? Could our praying be an act of intentional alignment and realignment? That is, in our prayer our vision of the kingdom purposes of God will be deepened and broadened; we will be drawn into the reality of Christ risen and now on the throne of the universe. And thus through our prayers we not only pray for the kingdom but also come to increasingly live within the kingdom, under the reign of Christ.

This last point is crucial. So frequently we pray as though God is passive and we are trying to get God to act. But could it be that God is always active? And that in our praying we are aware of how God is actually always at work, bringing his kingdom into effect, and we are seeing and responding to the kingdom even as we pray "thy kingdom come"? In the process, we are increasingly more aligned and in tune with the kingdom, more and more living our lives, individually and in community, in a manner that consistently reflects, in word and deed, the coming kingdom of God.

THREE MOVEMENTS IN OUR PRAYERS

Can we do this? Certainly, but only if we are intentional. We need to consider the merits of a very focused and purposeful approach to our prayers. Yes, there is a place for spontaneity. And most certainly there is a place for freeform prayers where we express to God our immediate thoughts and feelings. But when we speak of our formation in Christ and our participation in the kingdom—where the kingdom of God increasingly defines us more than anything else—we should perhaps be focused and purposeful. We can consider the value of consistency and even routine, an approach to prayer that has an order to it. We can even speak of a liturgy, meaning that our prayers have a regular pattern to them so that over time our hearts and minds and lives are increasingly conformed to the very thing for which we are praying.

In this kind of intentionality it is very helpful to think in terms of three movements in our prayers, three forms of prayer by which we respond to and learn to live in the reality that Christ is risen and active in our world—that in and through Christ the reign of God is coming. Three movements, with an intentional sequence.

First, we give thanks. We see and respond with gratitude to the ways in which God is already at work in our world and in our lives. We begin here. We begin by seeing the evidence of the reign of Christ—the ways that God is already at work in our lives and in our world. And we give thanks. We pray "thy kingdom come" in a way that not only acknowledges that God is already at work but celebrates and gives thanks for this work. We cannot pray "thy kingdom come" if we are not grateful for how the kingdom has come and is coming. Thanksgiving is foundational to the Christian life and thus foundational to prayer.

Second, we make confession—the essential realignment of those who long to live under the reign of Christ. We pray "thy kingdom come," and very soon we also pray—if we follow the sequence of the Lord's Prayer—"forgive us our debts, as we also have forgiven our debtors." We practice confession. It is clear from Scripture that when the kingdom is announced and when the kingdom is at hand—present, in our midst, and recognized—we respond with confession (Mark 1:15).

Confession is essential if we truly recognize and believe in the coming of the kingdom. If we have kingdom eyes, the genius of our response is that we see where there is a disconnect. We see and feel that our lives are not being lived in a way that is consistent with the kingdom. We cannot pray "your will be done, on earth as it is in heaven" unless and until we see the ways that our lives are not lived in consistency with the will of God. And so, recognizing the kingdom, we repent: we practice confession. Repentance, then, is not merely a matter of feeling bad about something we have said or done, but rather an act of intentional alignment—or better, *realignment*—with the coming of the reign of Christ.

And third, we practice discernment—considering where and how God is calling us to speak and act as participants in the kingdom of God. We pray "thy kingdom come" as those who are also called to be full participants, in word and deed, in what God is doing in the world. And so when we pray we of course ask—or better, *discern*—how we are called in our lives to witness to the kingdom.

We are not merely observers; we are engaged. We are invited—more, actually *called* as agents of God's purposes in the world. Our words *and* our deeds matter. In some mysterious way, even though God and God alone brings about the kingdom, our lives witness to the kingdom—our words, our work. And so when we pray "thy kingdom come," we also necessarily must pray, *How, oh Lord, are you calling me to make a difference in your kingdom purposes for our world?*

THREE TEMPTATIONS

Thanksgiving. Confession. Discernment. It may sound simple and straightforward, except for this: our hearts are not naturally inclined in this direction. Our default mode is not thanksgiving or confession or discernment. There is a powerful inclination that undercuts each of these—an orientation, a temptation that will keep us from praying well.

When it comes to thanksgiving, we so frequently focus on what God is *not* doing—on all the ways that we wish God were more present, more active, more attentive, actually doing what we wish God were doing but seems to not be doing. We see all that is wrong or lacking, and this is what most engages our hearts and minds.

But could it be that the genius of seeing well—of having kingdom eyes—is that we are first and foremost attentive to what God is *already* doing? Rather than complaint for what is wrong, our point of departure is thanksgiving for the multiple ways that God is indeed already at work. And we give thanks. We begin and end our day with thanksgiving rather than complaint. We develop kingdom eyes that can see and appreciate the sometimes very quiet and subtle ways that God is at work.

So frequently we bemoan the state of our circumstances or the state of our society and, ironically, miss the ways that God is at work in our midst. Yes, we do need to be agents of positive change, but could it be that we can only discern God's particular call on us now if we are able to see how God is already at work? Rather than looking to other societies where we are impressed that God is at work in seemingly miraculous and dramatic ways and bemoaning that this is not happening in our situation, should we not see that perhaps in a secularized society God may be working in a far more subtle way? Having kingdom eyes means that we can see and appreciate and give thanks for the ways that God is at work.

When it comes to confession, the temptation is to look at how others are falling short, how others are not living up to the kingdom. Whether it is the people we work with, the people we live with, or the people we worship with, we think of all the ways that *they* need to change.

In our work, it is so easy to spend our energy frustrated with others and wishing that others would change. And while there is surely a place for accountability within the workplace, we would do well to humbly see and recognize where God is calling us to turn, to repent.

It is so easy to be disappointed with those who are older or those who are younger—feeling that our parents' generation missed something or that the generation that follows us is not quite as committed or devoted as we are.

It is so easy to judge other church groups as somehow deficient, rather than asking and discerning how God is calling us to be more faithful to the gospel and repenting in response. And it is so easy to engage our society as critics and judges.

But the genius of confession is found in the immortal words of the psalmist: "Search me, O God. . . . See if there is any wicked way in me" (Psalm 139:23-24). The kingdom orientation is not to see the mote or speck in our neighbor's eye, but to see the beam in our own eye (Matthew 7:3). We let God do God's work in God's time in the other. We recognize that we cannot confess for the other. And we instead take responsibility for our lives, for our behavior. Thus, to pray "thy kingdom come" is to turn from complaint to thanksgiving, and it is also to turn from judging others to making personal confession.

Then we also ask, How are we being called to speak and to act in witness to the kingdom of God? We learn discernment. The temptation here is twofold. One temptation is to see all that is wrong with the world, decide that the situation is hopeless, and despair—to throw up our hands and conclude that nothing can be done or that nothing is worth doing. We allow the seeds of cynicism to be sown in our hearts. The other temptation is to try to do everything—to be heroes, little messiahs. We go through our days in frenetic busyness, overwhelmed by all that needs to be done and impatient with ourselves, with others, and of course with God, somehow thinking that by the sheer dint of our own efforts we can fix our circumstances and our world.

But is there not a third way? The way of quiet, even leisured, and courageous action, where we speak and act with wisdom, grace, and patience? Where we recognize that we are called to be players on God's stage and in the drama of God's kingdom purposes in the world, but with the deep and quiet knowledge and assurance that we are not the stars of the show? Can we let God be God and then also learn to speak and act in light of this: to be where are we being called to be and say what we are being called to say and do what we are being called to do? We are actors in God's work in the world as we witness in word and deed in all we do. But what we must stress is that we are truly actors only if we do that which we are *actually* called to do. No more; no less.

And this changes. As circumstances change in our personal lives and in our workplaces, or as changes come in our communities and societies, we need to ask afresh, *How, oh God, are you calling us, in this time and place and set of circumstances, to be participants in your kingdom?* We turn from despair to considered and courageous action; we turn from frenetic busyness and attend to that to which we have been called.

We practice thanksgiving. And we turn from complaint.

We practice confession. And we turn from a judgmental, critical spirit.

We practice discernment. And we turn from both despair and frenetic busyness.

Three movements in our praying: each is a vital and essential dimension of the prayer "thy kingdom come."

PRAYING IN THE SPIRIT

*i*n our prayers we are drawn into union with Christ, the ascended Lord. Through prayer, slowly but surely, our minds are set "on things that are above" (Colossians 3:2); our life is found—or, in the language of Colossians 3:3, "hidden"—with Christ. In other words, prayer is not merely a matter of a kingdom—a new sphere of reality and new perspective on life and work. Through prayer we are actually entering into fellowship with the one who reigns over this kingdom.

Yes, through prayer we come to love that which is consistent with the reign of Christ: our minds are set on the true, the honorable, the just, the pure, and that which is truly excellent (see Philippians 4:8). But more, we actually come to love Christ and delight in the one who is bringing about his kingdom purposes in the world. Christ himself becomes our true home.

In our prayers we transcend this earthly sphere of reality and live—that is, find our true home—in another sphere of reality. We do not discount the materiality of our world and our deep physical attachment to this earth. We are still very much here and very much engaged with the reality of the societies and cultures of which we are a part. But what defines our identity and our vision of reality is not this world but another world. We actually draw life, strength, vision, and grace from that which is unseen.

We are drawn into the life of the risen and ascended Christ, we are able to set our minds on things above, precisely and specifically as we learn to give thanks, make confession, and practice discernment. That is, the great call of John 15:4—"abide in me as I abide in you"—is fulfilled within us as we learn to pray.

PRAYER IN A SECULAR AGE

The assumption that there is another sphere of reality beyond what we can see and touch and taste and hear seems manifestly a contradiction to the dominant social, political, and cultural context in which we are being called to live out our Christian faith. We are living in and seeking to pray in societies that are increasingly secular, at a time that is aptly spoken of as "a secular age." We live in societies and communities where the Christian voice is no longer privileged: religious identity and values are consistently discounted. The tenor of public discourse is at best pluralist, but in fact, as often as not, religion is up against the hegemony, the default, of secular values and perspectives.

What does it mean to pray when the kingdoms of this world are front and center? And when the challenges of racism, consumerism, and genuine pluralism cry out for a Christian perspective? What does it mean to pray when materialism—the assumption that the only reality is that which you can taste and touch and see—is in the very air that we breathe?

It surely means that we learn to give thanks. Rather than constantly complaining about what we think the church has lost, we should be alert to the diverse and perhaps subtle ways in which God is very much active. Many Christians tend to assume that the rise of secularism is a very bad thing and wring their hands in despair that Christian values are no longer affirmed in the public square: for example, the loss of the Lord's Prayer in city council proceedings or the lack of a nativity crèche on the lawn of the state legislative building. But perhaps we let it go; perhaps we accept that this move toward secularism might actually be providential. Perhaps God intends a different vision for mission and witness in our day, and rather than fighting secularism we should ask what opportunities this opens up for Christian witness. And this means learning to give thanks for what God is doing uniquely and no less powerfully in this social context.

Praying in this age also means making confession rather than constantly judging those around us. What does holiness look like in this age? What are the sins that we most need to confront in ourselves if we are to be faithful to our calling?

Then, of course, discernment is doubly crucial: What are we called to say and do? What does it mean to be a Christian and a Christian community for such a time as this?

In all of this, what does it mean not only to give thanks and make confession and practice discernment but to do so as those who are increasingly drawn into union with Christ? How do we pray when the social and cultural context in which we live discounts any kind of religious sensibility?

DEPENDING ON THE SPIRIT

Can we pray in such a way that we are increasingly drawn into fellowship with Christ through thanksgiving, confession, and discernment? Can we turn from complaint, from a judgmental spirituality, and from either frenetic busyness or despair?

However tempting it is to say yes, we must acknowledge that this is actually beyond us. We are so easily distracted by all that is wrong and all that we wish were different. We are so easily aware of the shortcomings of others rather than our own faults. And we are so easily overcome by all that needs to be done or all that we think we should do or wish we could do.

But then we turn to the good news that, as Paul puts it, though we do not know how to pray, the Spirit prays with us: "Likewise the Spirit helps us in our weakness; for we do not know how to pray as we ought, but that very Spirit intercedes with sighs too deep for words. And God, who searches the heart, knows what is the mind of the Spirit, because the Spirit intercedes for the saints according to the will of God" (Romans 8:26-27). The Spirit is our advocate and counselor.

Indeed, we should beware of those who seem to imply that prayer is easy—we just speak to God. Just talk! Rather, we can acknowledge that we do not know how to pray. That when it comes to thanksgiving, confession, and discernment, we are as often as not at a loss for words.

But then we can turn to the one in whom and with whom we pray. We come to recognize that prayer should, perhaps, be something we do "in the Spirit." By this I mean nothing more than the intentionality of leaning into the Spirit, the intentionality whereby we ask for and learn how to recognize the prompting and guidance of the Spirit in our prayers. We need to get at what the apostle means by calling his readers to "pray in the Spirit at all times" (Ephesians 6:18). Indeed, I wonder whether this is one of the most crucial ways by which we learn to live by the Spirit and be led by the Spirit (to use the expressions of Paul in Galatians 5:16 and 18): to live by the Spirit is to be always *praying* in the Spirit.

So if we are going to pray the prayer "thy kingdom come," it would be wise and appropriate that we pray in intentional response to the presence and work of the Spirit in our lives and in our world. Prayer is not so much asking things of God as responding to the ways that the Spirit is inviting and leading us to pray "thy kingdom come." Prayer is an act of response to the initiative of God.

In our thanksgiving, we ask, *Oh Spirit of God, where are you inviting me, calling me, to give thanks? Help me to see what you see. Help me to see the subtle and yet powerful way in which you are doing your good work. Help me to be patient as you do what only you can do.* Even in the midst of a deeply fragmented world, there is so much for which we can give thanks. So much. We can declare, *I choose to turn from complaint, from seeing all that is wrong and lacking, and to acknowledge—even more, oh Spirit of God, to celebrate— how you are at work in our work, in our church, in our lives.*

In our confession, we ask the Spirit to come near: to humble our hearts that we might see the ways in which we are so easily self-deceived and so easily justify ourselves. We cannot make confession without the help of the Spirit. We need the gracious convicting ministry of the Spirit—so gentle yet firm, piercing yet compassionate—calling us, animating us, empowering us. As noted, we easily look at the shortcomings of others. The Spirit humbles us and fosters within us a penitential spirit, cutting against the grain of our judgmentalism and undercutting our proclivity toward spiritual pride.

And as we seek to discern how we are called to witness in word and deed to the kingdom, we lean into the Spirit, inviting the Spirit to illuminate our hearts and minds and give us clarity, direction, and courage. And we ask for humility— to do what we are called to do and accept what is not ours to do. We are overwhelmed and likely confused by all that needs to be done and could be done. We need clarity of heart and mind regarding where and how God is calling us to speak and act in our contexts, in the particulars of our lives. We need the guidance of the Spirit.

Our only hope for praying "thy kingdom come" as those who live within a dominant secular society and culture is to learn what it means to pray in the Spirit so that in the Spirit we are setting our minds on things above, where our lives are hidden with Christ.

When we pray "thy kingdom come," we should very intentionally pray in the Spirit. We will ask the Spirit to draw to our attention, to move our hearts to recognize that which we should give thanks and that which we should confess. We will be Spirit dependent in our prayers. We will give priority to the Spirit and in our praying grow in our capacity for vocational discernment—acting in the world in response to the specific calling and inner witness of the Spirit.

Praying in the Spirit means that in our prayers we listen twice as much as we speak. We attend to the Spirit, and the Spirit takes the lead. We are responding more than we are initiating. We learn to be attentive to how the Spirit is guiding and directing us in our prayers.

It is important to stress that praying in the Spirit is a learned art. It comes naturally to no one. Further, it requires a settled and centered heart and mind. We need to slow down and learn how to recognize the witness of the Spirit, which is often quiet and understated. Elijah learned that the Lord was not in the earthquake, the wind, or the fire, but in the sound of still silence (1 Kings 19:11-12). We learn to recognize the prompting of the one who, as a rule, does not shout and whose guidance of our hearts will, more often than not, come through a subtle inner witness.

It is no wonder then that when it comes to discernment, it takes time to develop kingdom eyes. In the words of the early church and medieval spiritual masters, we come to recognize that the Spirit's guidance comes in consolation, not desolation. But more, we learn that the Spirit guides those whose fundamental disposition of heart is marked by two things: gratitude and penitence. Both thanksgiving and repentance are acts by which we come to know the ordering of the affections. And the sequence from thanksgiving to confession to discernment is important. We learn how to discern well by coming to discernment with a grateful and penitential disposition.

And so why would this not be the approach we take to our daily prayers? Each day, preferably early in the day, accompanied by meditative engagement with the Scriptures, we would ask the Spirit to guide our prayers and would give thanks as the Spirit guides us. We would make confession in response to the convicting work of the Spirit. And we would practice discernment for the day and the days that are before us, seeking guidance and insight into the challenges and opportunities we will be facing. We pray, each day, in the Spirit.

THE PSALMS AND OUR PRAYERS

If we are going to pray in the Spirit, our prayers need to be grounded in and guided by the prayer book of the Bible. The Psalms are the historically proven means by which the Spirit fosters our capacity to pray, bringing our hearts and minds into alignment with the reign of Christ. I write about prayer out of a deep conviction that we need to allow the Old Testament Psalms to inform our prayers—and to more often than not actually make the Psalms our prayers. We learn to pray by praying the Psalms. We come back to them again and again and recognize in time that all of our prayers are but echoes of the Psalms. The Psalms are the invaluable and essential resource that is given to each of us—and to the church—so that we can truly pray "thy kingdom come."

We pray Psalm 145:10-13, for example, in which we speak of our deep delight in the kingdom of God:

> All your works shall give thanks to you, O LORD,
>   and all your faithful shall bless you.
> They shall speak of the glory of your kingdom,
>   and tell of your power,
> to make known to all people your mighty deeds,
>   and the glorious splendor of your kingdom.
> Your kingdom is an everlasting kingdom,
>   and your dominion endures throughout all
>   generations.

We delight in the kingdom, and through the Psalms we nurture a longing for the kingdom. We grow to appreciate—again, through the Psalms—that the kingdom matters more than anything else to us. It is our deep longing and yearning.

From the church fathers and through the witness of virtually every spiritual master in the history of the church, we come to appreciate that the Psalms are not incidental to our prayers

and to the church's worship but fundamental and essential. As
Christians, we learn to pray by praying the Psalms. As the
church, in our weekly worship we learn to pray and to worship
by praying the Psalms.

The Psalms provide us with the fundamental orientation
of thanksgiving and praise as we celebrate and give thanks to
the God who is Creator and Redeemer. Every Psalm celebrates the work of God as either Creator or Redeemer, or in
many cases, both. The Psalms also provide the structure and
form that are needed for our penitential prayers, giving direction and substance to our confession, and also the assurance of God's mercy and pardon.

Further, the Psalms provide us with a rich vision of reality
that can and must inform our prayers of discernment. They
give us words that can foster an emotional honesty and maturity; there is nothing here of "happy-clappy" worship.
Rather, the full spectrum of human affect and emotion, including lament, finds expression in the Psalms. And this kind
of emotional forthrightness—everything from anger to joyful
ecstasy—is essential if we are to discern well. In other words,
the blunt honesty of the Psalms about the evil and fragmentation in the world fosters within us a capacity to discern in
light of this reality rather than be naive to the presence and
power of evil in our world and, of course, in our own hearts.

In learning to pray the Psalms we find that they are the very
means by which the Spirit draws us into fellowship with
Christ. Also, the Psalms are the means by which the Spirit

brings us into fellowship with the community of faith—the people of God. And further, as we pray the Psalms, the whole of the Scriptures is brought into our consciousness by the Spirit.

With regard to fellowship with Christ, these are the prayers of Christ—all the Psalms, not just those that are clearly messianic. The "king" in the Psalms is, for Christians, the one who reigns over the kingdom of God. Thus in praying the Psalms we are drawn into fellowship with Christ and with the purposes of Christ for the world. We come to see the world as Christ sees it. We come to both an understanding and an affective awareness—that is, our hearts are aligned with the heart of Christ. We can certainly pray the Psalms as our prayers. But they are our prayers because they are the prayers of Christ, and we are found in Christ.

Then also, the Psalms are not so much personal prayers as the prayer book of the people of Israel and Jesus and thus of the church. These are the prayers of the church, and in praying them we are praying with God's people of all generations and cultures. Whether the Psalms are prayed together on Sunday—heard, sung, said antiphonally—or in the privacy of our own solitary prayers, we are still praying with the church, in fellowship with the church. Thus in praying the Psalms we cut against any propensity we might have toward a purely solitary faith—a faith that is not sustainable. Even when we pray alone we pray as those who are in fellowship with God's people, and this is particularly evident when we pray the Psalms.

Finally, in praying the Psalms we are drawn into the Word of God. We learn to delight in the law, in truth—as described, for example, in Psalms 19 and 119, which are extended anthems of praise to the Torah, the Law of God. Thus as we pray the Psalms our hearts are formed and transformed. Our desires are purified. Our affections, to use ancient language, are ordered. Increasingly, heart and mind and soul are aligned with Christ himself, with his people, and with his Word. When we pray the Psalms we are fulfilling something of what was intended in the call of the apostle to let the word of Christ dwell richly within us (Colossians 3:16).

OUR PRAYERS AND THE EUCHARIST

As we speak of prayer we need to also consider the celebration of the Lord's Supper. One of the primary ways by which the Spirit does the Spirit's work in our lives is through the sacramental actions of the church. We cannot speak of the ministry of the Spirit in our lives without at some point speaking of the Eucharist. This is so for at least two reasons.

First, our personal prayers need to reflect and arise out of our participation in the prayers of the community of faith. We read that the early Christian community, following the day of Pentecost, "devoted themselves to the apostles' teaching and fellowship, to the breaking of bread and the prayers" (Acts 2:42). It is imperative to stress, if we are going to pray in the Spirit, that the Spirit is the one who draws Christians together for worship. And the ministry of the Word and the sacrament of the Lord's Table are foundational to Christian worship. We are not in fellowship with the Spirit, in our prayers or in any respect, if we are not in fellowship with the church. Our prayers are the prayers of those who pray in solitude, of course, but also the prayers of those who pray with the church—the church that is a community that devotes itself to Word and sacrament.

Second, the celebration of the Eucharist is a fundamentally physical act—tangible and embodied. In the celebration of the Lord's Table we are very much worshiping in and with our bodies, eating together and drinking together. This is noteworthy for a number of reasons, but in speaking of prayer in particular it is helpful to highlight one implication: there is a twofold danger in our prayers. One danger is that our prayers would be entirely a cerebral, mental exercise—we *think* about God and *think* about the kingdom of God. The other danger is any proclivity toward sentimentality. This means our prayers would be nothing other than nice feelings— presumably about God and about God's purposes in our lives and in our world, but in the end nothing but sentiment. These are good feelings, but they are not that which leads to either our transformation or the fostering of our capacity to truly engage our world.

Our hearts and minds are crucial to our prayers; we worship and pray as those with engaged intellects and with open and attentive hearts. We urgently need worship with God's people and in our personal prayers that is deeply informed by a theological vision for the kingdom of God. Thus in affirming the place of the Eucharist I am not for a moment discounting the importance of intellectual engagement. At the same time, not for a moment should we minimize the vital place of a heartfelt engagement with God—the God who loves us and grants us, through the Spirit, an affective awareness of Christ's presence in our lives.

But prayer that is either purely cerebral or purely sentimental is not, in the end, transformative. We are embodied souls, and if the grace and presence of God is not ultimately embodied, if it does not happen in our bodies, it does not happen. Indeed, what allows us to pray with heart and mind—with the integration of heart and mind—is specifically that we pray in our bodies.

And thus we need all the classic physical gestures of prayer—including the act of kneeling and even prostration and the lifting up of our hands in gratitude and praise. But most of all we need the Eucharist as the supreme act by which we bring our bodies into the presence of the ascended Lord, who hosts us at the table.

Each dimension of prayer—thanksgiving, confession, and discernment—connects with an aspect of the Lord's Supper. We can think of how the Lord's Supper is thanksgiving (Eucharist); and how the Lord's Supper is, through confession, a table of mercy; and how through discernment we find food for the road—renewed hope and nourishment for the work and witness to which we are called. That is, we can come to appreciate that to pray in the Spirit means not some kind of disembodied prayer but rather the prayer of those who meet with Christ, in real time, at the table.

THE EVIDENCE THAT WE ARE PRAYING IN THE SPIRIT

When all is said and done, how will we know this is happening? What will be the evidence that we are indeed praying in the Spirit?

First, *character*. We grow in faith, hope, and love; we know and live in the holiness of God. That is, if we are praying in the Spirit, it will be evident in the quality of our lives—in our increased capacity to live lives marked by moral intelligence and wisdom. The reign of Christ, the authority of Christ, will increasingly be evident in the way in which we live and work and in the quality of our relationships. Our prayers will actually be a means of our formation.

Second, *vocational clarity and patience*. Those who pray in the Spirit as I am suggesting are those who say what needs to be said and do what needs to be done. They do not overspeak, they are not overly wordy, they are good listeners. They are at peace to be silent or quiet, and yet they know what it is to "make an apt answer . . . a word in season" (Proverbs 15:23). They also do what they are called to do—no more, no less. They are able to make difficult decisions with an awareness of the deep ambiguities of life, yet with a certain decisiveness. It may strike us as self-confidence, but it is better to describe is as nothing more than the humility to do what needs to be done and say what needs to be said. These people act without frenetic busyness or despair or frustration that they do not have the time they need.

That is the genius of it, actually: women and men who pray in the Spirit do what they are called to do, even if it involves very difficult decisions, with a gracious courage and patience. There is no other way to describe it than as the grace of being patient. Patience is not acquiescence. It is the twin to decisive and courageous words and deeds.

Third, those who pray in the Spirit are marked by a resilient *joy.* Joy is not mere sentimentality or an optional extra. In many respects it is the heart of the matter—not of secondary significance in the Christian journey. It is the joy of alignment: Why would it not be the case that as we live increasingly in alignment with the reign of Christ we come to know what it means that Christ Jesus has come so that our joy may be complete (John 15:11)? We will encounter much sorrow and suffering in this world. And yet, in the midst of it all, joy will be our true home, the fundamental orientation and disposition of our hearts and lives. And fear will dissipate.

This is only possible, of course, because we know that evil does not have the last word—that indeed the kingdom will come and Christ will reign and will, in due time, make all things well. Yes, we are participants in the kingdom of God now, but what we see and experience will without doubt be marked by much that falls short of ideal. Many come to the end of their lives and their careers deeply disappointed with God and with others. But those who pray in the Spirit are marked by an uncanny joy—largely because they know that what is before them is not the last word and that when all is said and done the kingdom of God will come.

So frequently we think that if we have conviction and ideals—for the church, for our institutions, and for our families, including our children—this strength of vision for all that could be, and in our minds *should* be, will be evident in our impatience with people and with systems (which is another way of saying "people"). We think that our disappointment with how things are is a sign of moral and intellectual strength. Yet those who pray in the Spirit, while they are deeply engaged and without doubt keenly feel all that is not what it should be, are not robbed of joy. Their joy is a reflection of their quiet assurance of the ultimate coming of the reign of Christ.

Finally, the key indicator that we are praying in the Spirit is *humility*. As discussed in chapter one, there are three major temptations that we come up against in our prayers: the temptation to complain rather than give thanks, the temptation to judge rather than make personal confession, and the temptation to either frenetic busyness or despair rather than the way of discernment. And yet in the end there is only one temptation: that we would view ourselves as somehow at the center of the universe. So easily our default mode is of living as though everything revolved around us.

But when we pray "thy kingdom come," what essentially happens is that we recognize the priority of the kingdom. Thus we learn to see all things, including our lives, through the lens of the reality of the reign of Christ and the kingdom of God. And this necessarily means that we grow in freedom and humility. Increasingly, Christ is the center of our universe, and we find freedom in no longer needing to be at the center.

Humility is nothing other than to know and experience ourselves in truth, in freedom, with Christ and the reign of Christ as all that truly consumes us. We are not obsessed or consumed with ourselves but with the reign of Christ. Our prayers are not all about us. Sure, our own context and life situation is without doubt the lens by which we come to Christ and pray "thy kingdom come." But as the Spirit guides us in our prayers, they will be defined not by the particulars of our lives but rather, first and foremost, by our longing for the reign of Christ. Yes, our prayers are about us, but they are about us in *light* of the kingdom. Thus when we pray for ourselves and for the needs and longings that inevitably arise in our lives, it is not because we are overly concerned with ourselves. It is actually because we long for our lives to be found within and under and in light of the reign of Christ. And this is freedom. The freedom to let God be God: to find deep joy in not presuming or desiring to be God.

THE PRAYER OF
THANKSGIVING

*i*n our prayers and in our worship, few things are so crucial as this: that the disposition of our hearts and the words of our mouths are marked by a deep and *insistent* gratitude. I say "insistent" because without intentionality and persistence on this point we will find that complaint and disappointment will too easily be the defining markers of our lives.

FOR GOD IS GOOD

We give thanks, we bless the name of the Lord—as the psalmist declares—because God is good.

> Enter his gates with thanksgiving,
>   and his courts with praise.
>   Give thanks to him, bless his name.
> For the LORD is good;
>   his steadfast love endures forever,
>   and his faithfulness to all generations. (Psalm 100:4-5)

God is good, and his love endures forever. Everything in the Christian life presumes this fundamental conviction and point of departure: the goodness of God. God is on our side; God is for us and not against us; indeed, God is good.

In recent years it has become common for Christian congregations to affirm their faith not only with the ancient creeds and with hymns that celebrate God as Creator and Redeemer, but also through a very simple and yet very powerful affirmation that goes like this:

> Worship leader: *God is good!*
> Congregational response: *All the time!*
> Worship leader: *All the time . . .*
> Congregational response: *God is good!*

This is truly a baseline, a fundamental and thus essential affirmation of our faith. The faith of the Christian community rests on this conviction: the providential goodness of God.

And this finds parallel expression in our personal prayers. Ignatius Loyola, in his classic guide to prayer, *The Spiritual Exercises*, stresses the need for the prayer of thanksgiving—for very specifically contemplating the love of God. It is from reading Ignatius that I have come to appreciate that when we give thanks, it is essential that we are particular—that is, we give *particular* thanks for the *particular* way in which God has been good to us. We make it personal: I give thanks for how God has been good to me.

This is not narcissism or self-centeredness. Rather, it is a recognition that the only way I can know and affirm that God is good is to affirm the ways in which God has been good to me personally. Children will immediately protest if they feel that their parents are good to their siblings but not to them, and they will respond with a firm "Unfair!" If we think God is good to others and not to us, we do not really believe that God is truly good. We truly know and feel the goodness of God only as we engage it, experience it, and appreciate it in the particularity of our own lives. We only believe that God is good if we believe that God is good to us.

And therefore it follows that in our prayers we speak to the goodness of God and give thanks for the specific and particular ways in which the goodness of God has intersected our lives.

BELABORING THE POINT

About midway through the book of Colossians we read,

> And let the peace of Christ rule in your hearts, to which indeed you were called in the one body. And be thankful. Let the word of Christ dwell in you richly; teach and admonish one another in all wisdom; and with gratitude in your hearts sing psalms, hymns, and spiritual songs to God. And whatever you do, in word or deed, do everything in the name of the Lord Jesus, giving thanks to God the Father through him. (Colossians 3:15-17)

The apostle belabors the point: three times in three verses he calls for thanksgiving. I jokingly think to myself, *He obviously did not have to work with editors like those who review drafts of my manuscripts.* They would likely urge him to make the point once, or at most twice, and let it be! But he clearly is very intentional in making this point again and yet again.

In verse 15 he just says, "And be thankful." Basic, simple, and straightforward. Hard to miss. But then in verse 16 he emphasizes that worship is to be offered with gratitude: in teaching and admonition, and in song, Christian worship is to be offered by grateful people. And then, lest we still have not gotten the point, he covers the whole landscape, the whole of our lives: everything, whatever is said and whatever is done, is to be done with thanksgiving. Each of these three verses stresses this call to live with thanksgiving as the animating dynamic of our lives.

This should come as no surprise, given the emphasis on thanksgiving in the whole of the biblical witness. Gratitude is central to the Christian life. Indeed, earlier in the book of Colossians the apostle urges his readers, having "received Christ Jesus the Lord," to continue to be rooted in Christ and maturing in Christ (Colossians 2:6-7)—the maturity toward which Paul himself is so eagerly working (Colossians 1:28). Then they will grow and mature as they have been taught, as they are "abounding in thanksgiving" (Colossians 2:7). This suggests that there is no growth in the spiritual life, no maturity, without gratitude.

THE GRATEFUL CHRISTIAN

We only pray well when we give thanks. But this assumes that the Christian life is lived from a posture of thankfulness—that indeed this is what it means to be a Christian.

This has been brought home to me at several key turning points in my life. I remember one instance when I was a teen in the back seat of our car as our family returned home from a trip to the coast. My mother, as was her pattern, spoke the words "Thank God for traveling mercies" as we pulled into our driveway. I pointed out, with classic teenage wisdom, that there were thousands of cars on the road that day, so why should we presume that somehow the hand of God was upon our particular vehicle, guiding us along? Her response was poignant and timely: "Oh Gordon, yes indeed, the mercy and goodness of God is very much on each of the cars and trucks along the road. The difference is that Christians give thanks."

That line, "Christians give thanks," came back to me several years later when as a university student on a break from my formal studies I spent some time at a study center in Huémoz, Switzerland, known as L'Abri Fellowship. Founded and led by Francis and Edith Schaeffer, this was a safe place for many like myself who were wandering around Europe with some vague sense that we were trying to find ourselves.

While I was there, Francis Schaeffer was preaching a series of sermons on the book of Romans. I now read the book of Romans quite differently from Schaeffer, but in his preaching on Romans 1 he made a point that has stayed with me ever since. He leaned over the podium and urged us to feel the force of Romans 1:21, which speaks of the refusal to honor God, but very specifically to give thanks to God. Schaeffer, with the full force of his personality, urged us to see this: the essence of paganism is the refusal to give thanks. The Christian, he stressed, gives thanks. With minimal eloquence, but no less effectively, he virtually shouted at us: *Be grateful!*

Some years later, I was a pastor of a small congregation in Peterborough, Ontario. It was not only a relatively small congregation, but it was also a rather conflicted, troubled, and underwhelming expression of Christian community. For my first year in this pastoral post, I became more and more aware, week to week, of all the limitations and problems of this congregation to which I had been assigned. And then, almost exactly a year into this ministry, I discovered and read through Dietrich Bonhoeffer's masterful guide to the spiritual life, *Life Together*.

In this remarkable essay, Bonhoeffer also stresses how crucial thanksgiving is to the Christian life, and particularly to life in community. He observes that we do not enter into community as demanders but rather as grateful recipients. Then, speaking specifically to pastors and religious leaders, he is particularly firm in his insistence that we do not have the option of complaint regarding—in my case—the congregation where I served as pastor. He considers this to be a particularly egregious case of ingratitude. And then he writes that unless we are grateful for what God has already given us, we cannot expect that God will entrust us with more.

That turn of phrase is crucial. We can only move into what God has for us if we are grateful for what is already in our lives, already a reflection of God's providential care. This is not to suggest that in being grateful we are entitled to more—not for a moment. It means, rather, that to pray without gratitude is presumption. And gratitude—whether I learned it from my mother or from Schaeffer or from Bonhoeffer—remains fundamental: to be a Christian is to be a grateful person.

GIVING THANKS IN THE SPIRIT

If we are going to be grateful people, we need to appreciate that this will happen—it will be the pattern and disposition and habit of the heart—only if we begin with our prayers. We must learn to enter into prayer with thanksgiving, learn how to give intentional and informed thanksgiving in our worship with the people of God and in our personal prayers.

And this means, I would stress, we must pray with thanksgiving again and again and again; we do it as habit, as pattern, as the very rhythm of our lives. We do it weekly when we gather for worship with our church community; we do it daily in our personal prayers. The deep disposition of gratitude, as a fundamental and defining orientation of our lives, will come only as we make this a practice—quite literally, a routine.

We can truly do this, given the inclination of our hearts, only if we make it a practice to "pray in the Spirit at all times" and on all occasions (Ephesians 6:18). In the Spirit we persist in giving thanks.

And it makes sense to be intentional in this regard—in our praying to consciously attend to the ways in which the Spirit is inviting us, if not actually urging us, to give thanks. We pray, *Oh Spirit of God, guide me in my prayers and draw to my attention those dimensions of my life that reflect your goodness. Help me to see, in the midst of all that strikes me as wrong and so not what I would like it to be, the particular ways in which you are demonstrating your goodness.*

This kind of praying does not ignore or deny what is wrong. When in our prayers we give thanks, we are not for a moment discounting the reality of evil in our lives and in our world. We are rather affirming that even when so much is so very wrong, we are confident that good will triumph over evil. We affirm that our inner orientation and disposition is not toward what is—the present evil—but what will be—the triumph of the goodness of God.

This is a supreme act of faith: to give thanks in the midst of a fallen and broken world, to realize and affirm that God never leaves himself without a witness to his fundamental goodness. It may be slight; it may be nothing more than the light that shines through the crack in the prison wall. But the signs—the reminders—are always there: God is good. Thus, confident of the future, we can be present to the indicators of God's goodness in the midst of our circumstances. We recognize that each indicator, great or small, is a sign of the providential care of God. And so we give thanks.

In praying in the Spirit, we are asking the Spirit to give us keen peripheral vision. It is so very easy for our hearts and minds to see only the wrong and even to be consumed or obsessed with all that is wrong. The wrong is real, and it must be addressed. But we will be able to be positive agents for God and for the kingdom only if our fundamental disposition is one wherein we see and recognize the goodness of God and give thanks.

And thus we pray, *Oh Spirit of God, grant me eyes to see and appreciate and affirm where and how God has been good to me.* We do not assume that we have the internal or spiritual capacity to see the goodness of God. We rather recognize that we are dependent, necessarily leaning into the Spirit who guides us and prays with us and gives us kingdom eyes.

DWELLING IN THE LOVE OF GOD

When we pray in the Spirit, giving thanks, something happens. And there seems no other way to speak of this than as the opening up of the heart; there is a kind of loosening of the emotional contours of our lives. We become more tenderhearted. Those who complain as their pattern of being tend to be hardhearted—not so much distant or aloof, though in some cases that is how it might come across, and not introverted or shy, but rather hard. They have an edge, and the longer they have lived, the more it is clear that any personal warmth they have is skin deep. Warmth is not their essence.

But when as the pattern of our lives we give thanks—in the Spirit—as our way of being and our way of prayer, our hearts open. And the Scriptures remind us that "hope does not disappoint us, because God's love has been poured into our hearts through the Holy Spirit that has been given to us" (Romans 5:5). We feel—there is no better word for it—we *feel* the love of God: not as something that is superficial or tangential to our lives, but as part of the very fabric of our identity, our way of being. We are loved ones.

The psalmist urges us to give thanks, for God is good and his love endures forever. What we find is that in giving thanks, our encounter with the goodness and love of God is not purely cerebral; it is not and cannot be merely something we know or understand. Rather, we "get" this because it has filled us; we are bathed in and now sustained by the affective awareness of the love of God. It is surely this to which Jesus speaks when he says of his disciples that they will abide in him when they abide in his love (John 15:9).

Thus it is not too much to say that those who pray in the Spirit, giving thanks as the routine and pattern of their lives, will be women and men who are in relationship with others, do their work, and manage their daily chores and the challenges of life with a deep consciousness that they are loved. And they love others in like manner as they have been loved (see 1 John 4:9-11; John 15:12).

This awareness of the love of God is not something that leads to pride or self-centeredness for the very simple reason that these people know that they deserve nothing and have earned nothing. It is all gift. And thus there is a lightness and a freedom about them. The joy of knowing that one is loved is powerfully liberating. They do not need to impress anyone; they do not need to fear failure or even criticism. They are loved.

The point is that this conscious, affective awareness of the love of God is the fruit of a simple yet profound practice: giving thanks.

THANKSGIVING AND SUFFERING

But then, of course, we need to consider what it means to give thanks when there is so much that might put in question the goodness of God: suffering, pain, setbacks, and disappointment. How do we give thanks for the particular goodness of God when darkness and wrong intersect our lives?

In response, we must begin by affirming that nothing is gained by sentimentality or denial. The Psalms are a reminder to us, again and again, that God can handle our protest when we cry out, asking why God would allow something that is fundamentally wrong to happen. We also see this with particular force in the prayer of the Old Testament prophet Habakkuk. The whole of this book of the Bible is, essentially, a prayer—a prayer of stunning boldness in which Habakkuk opens with a plea for clarification. Why, he asks, does God seemingly stand by idly while an evil army runs rampant over the people of God? Does God tolerate evil and injustice?

The response from God, through the prophet himself, is
that God is deeply committed to righteousness and justice
and that in due time good will come. Thus, in the end the
prophet declares that even though what he longs for will not
happen right away, he will trust and rejoice in the God of his
salvation (Habakkuk 3:18). Habakkuk comes to us as a
prophet with a deep and resilient joy, a deep confidence in the
ultimate goodness of God. But he comes by that joy honestly.

Prayers of lament and prayers of thanksgiving are not mu-
tually exclusive. Yes, they are different. But the testimony of
Habakkuk and the numerous psalms of lament indicate that
lament at the deep fragmentation of the world and at our
own experience of deep wrong is not only a legitimate prayer
but also the very context in which we come to our thanksgiving. We lament, in part, because we know that God
is good.

Further, our thanksgiving is not an act of compliance or
naiveté regarding the wrongs of the world. We are not
thanking God for evil; just as assuredly, we are not ignoring
the evil around us. We will act; in our prayers we will discern
the appropriate response. But we will come to our discernment and thus our response from a deep consciousness
of the fundamental goodness of God and knowledge that
ultimately this goodness will be manifested in our world.

Thus we should be concerned about liturgies or approaches
to worship that have no lament, no place for perplexity, doubt,
and even anger. There is a powerful genius to such hymns as

"It Is Well with My Soul," with the extraordinary line "when sorrows like sea billows roll." My point is that God can handle this kind of honesty, this capacity for emotional disclosure. And it is not true joy and thus not true thanksgiving when we are not able to recognize that our thanks and praise to God and our affirmation of the goodness of God come with a full awareness of the deep fragmentation of our world and the ways in which that fragmentation intersects our individual lives.

We do not give thanks for evil. What is wrong is wrong. But we can give thanks in the midst of evil, and we can give thanks to a God who is able to bring good from evil. We can give thanks to a God for whom Good Friday is God's staggering identification with the evil of this world. And we can say this knowing that Good Friday is not the last word. Easter is coming.

Our thanksgiving in times of darkness and suffering will without doubt come more slowly and hesitantly. But it must come. Romans 5:3-4 states that suffering leads to endurance and endurance to character and character to hope. It is an amazing sequence and a reminder that women and men of hope are not necessarily those who have suffered little. Perseverance through suffering and the formation of character lead to hope. And yet we all know that this is not a given. For many, suffering leads to bitterness and anger and cynicism, the very opposite of hope. What is the difference? Surely it is the resolve and the capacity to give thanks even in, if not specifically in, the midst of suffering. That is, even when the way is dark—perhaps with sickness, personal or of a family member or friend, or significant challenges in the workplace—we have an attentive peripheral vision wherein we are not consumed by the problem before us but aware of the expressions of God's goodness to the right or the left.

Surely this is the critical evidence that we are grateful and that we believe in the goodness of God: that we learn to give thanks in the midst of suffering. We recognize that however dark and difficult a situation might be, God never leaves himself without a witness to goodness. We cling to this; we live here. We refuse to allow for the edge of bitterness or cynicism to take root in our hearts. We give thanks, and, in the exquisite words of Romans 5:5, "hope does not disappoint us, because God's love has been poured into our hearts through the Holy Spirit that has been given to us."

In many ways, this is the heart of the matter: Can we and will we give thanks—in the quietness of our own prayers and with the people of God in shared worship—even when our situation is dark? As noted, it may not come quickly or easily. But it must come. Our souls depend on this: that we sustain a willing and tender heart, a grateful heart.

THANKSGIVING AND THE EUCHARIST

When it comes to this resolve to be a grateful person, come what may, few things are so formative in the life of the church and of the individual Christian as the Lord's Table, appropriately called the *Eucharist*—the table of thanksgiving. Our prayers of thanksgiving bring us to this holy meal.

The apostle Paul speaks of the Lord's Supper as a table of blessing (1 Corinthians 10:16)—meaning a table of thanksgiving. In my experience growing up, when we gathered for the Lord's Supper we all knew the drill: one of the lay elders would pray a prayer of thanks for the bread, and then the bread was served. Then another elder would offer a prayer of thanks for the cup and for the shed blood of Christ. In retrospect it all seems rather quaint, and yet this really is the heart of the matter: we come to this table with thanksgiving.

Thus, for example, the preface to the Eucharist in the Book of Common Prayer reflects language that is also found in other older liturgies:

> *Presider*: The Lord be with you.
> *People*: And with thy spirit.
> *Presider*: Lift up your hearts.
> *People*: We lift them up unto the Lord.
> *Presider*: Let us give thanks unto the Lord our God.
> *People*: It is meet and right so to do.

The *sursum corda*—the invitation of the one presiding at the table, "Lift up your hearts"—is echoed in the call "Let us give thanks unto the Lord our God." How do we lift up our hearts to the Lord so that, in turn, the love of God is poured into our hearts (Romans 5:5)? By giving thanks. Thanksgiving is the very means by which we enter into the presence of Christ with open and attentive hearts and minds.

And then older liturgies or contemporary liturgies that draw on the wisdom of the early church also rightly include a Great Thanksgiving. Thus the celebration of this meal is located within the praise and thanksgiving that the church offers for all of God's gifts, including the greatest gift of all: God's very self in the person of his Son.

From beginning to end, the meal is a Eucharist—thanksgiving enacted. At this table we move into praise and adoration through the simple yet profound gestures of eating and drinking in the presence of Christ. In the act of eating and drinking we give thanks. Thanksgiving is then not merely something we think and say. And it is not merely a matter of heartfelt sentiments. It is embodied. We eat and drink, and our "eucharist," our sacrifice of praise and thanksgiving, *becomes* us. It is bred in our bones. If you want to become a grateful person, then join God's people in the prayer of thanksgiving and the act of thanksgiving that is the Lord's Supper.

When the way is dark, we will typically find that the feeling of gratitude is hard to come by. It can be difficult to say "thank you." Sometimes all we can do is come to the Lord's Table. We come in the company of others, and in humility we accept the gift of God's self to us and receive this gift with whatever faith we have and whatever measure of gratitude we can offer. Even if we cannot say "thank you" and can hardly feel gratitude, we still give thanks when we come to the Table.

FROM ENTITLEMENT TO GRATITUDE

On the Camino de Santiago de Compostela, the ancient pilgrimage route from southwestern France to northwestern Spain, there are, of course, pilgrims. But there are also tourists—those who are walking for any number of reasons, perhaps on the pathway for no other reason than curiosity. For such tourists the Camino is a matter of interest, but not a spiritual quest.

It is said that those along the way, who host the pilgrims in hotels and hostels and eateries, know the difference. They can tell who on the route is a tourist and who is a pilgrim. And the difference? A pilgrim gives thanks.

We give thanks out of a resolve that a spirit of entitlement will not mark our lives or invade our hearts. We will go through life knowing that all is gift. And so we give thanks—as a habit of the heart and something central to our practice of prayer.

THE PRAYER OF
CONFESSION

We pray, "thy kingdom come." And then we pray, "forgive us our debts." We move from the prayer for the kingdom to the prayer of confession. There is no other way to pray "thy kingdom come," and there is no other way to live under the reign of Christ. The two prayers are coupled.

If we pray in the Spirit, it necessarily means that we make confession. The Spirit invariably draws us to Christ, the living and ascended Lord, and enables us to see the disconnects in our lives—where and in what ways they are not lived under the authority of Christ. In the Spirit, everything—every aspect of our lives—must be brought under the dynamic and benevolent authority of Christ. Only then are we truly living out life in the kingdom; only then are we truly healed; only then are we genuinely saved. This is an inexorable process—however gentle the Spirit might be, however much the Spirit is the mother of our souls, the process is unrelenting. The Spirit does not rest until we find our rest in God. The love of God in Christ through the Spirit is so keen for our well-being that the Spirit will do what the Spirit must do: draw us to Christ and thus under the authority of Christ. For only under this authority do we know life, healing, and transformation. The apostle Paul states that what God has started, God will accomplish: "The one who began a good work among you will bring it to completion" (Philippians 1:6). This is truly the agenda of the Spirit.

It is no surprise, then, that Jesus announces, "The kingdom of God has come near," and then immediately calls for repentance: "repent, and believe in the good news" (Mark 1:15). It makes complete sense that on the day of Pentecost Peter insists that those who have responded positively to his message should "repent, and be baptized," with baptism in this situation clearly a penitential act (Acts 2:38).

Many within the evangelical spiritual and religious heritage have dispensed with prayers of confession, viewing them as almost a distraction from—if not an unpleasant intrusion into—joy-filled praise and worship. Unfortunately, these people have lost a sense of how confession is an essential element in Christian worship and thus necessarily integral to personal prayer. They have failed to appreciate that there is no spiritual growth—no spiritual maturity—without a dynamic rhythm of learning, understanding, and confession, with confession as the actual leverage point in moving us toward wisdom and holiness. By dismissing prayers of confession, we have removed from our worship one of the key means by which a person grows in faith, hope, and love. We have taken away an essential gateway to knowing the joy of God.

All of this assumes that the kingdom of God—the reign of Christ—is something for which we long, something we pursue; it is the dynamic focus of our hearts and minds. We seek the kingdom (Matthew 6:33). More to the point, we lean in and ask that the Spirit would equip and empower and convict and heal, that our lives would be a living expression of the good, the noble, the excellent, and the praiseworthy (see Philippians 4:8). We long for the beauty of the kingdom of God to infuse our imaginations and inform our vision of the world and our vision for human flourishing.

If we seek the kingdom of God, we will view the law of God with delight—not as a cruel taskmaster but as life giving. As an auto mechanic takes delight in a classic car that purrs like a cat, or a winemaker creates a perfect blend working with the grapes from a particularly good year, or a concert pianist performs Beethoven's Piano Concerto No. 4 with faithful attention to the composer, we see the law as our delight. Part of the power of effective preaching is that through the proclaimed Word God's people come to delight in the kingdom and grow in their appreciation for the beauty of the law. They come to see that joy is found in living in this law:

Happy are those whose way is blameless,
who walk in the law of the LORD.

Happy are those who keep his decrees,
> who seek him with their whole heart. (Psalm 119:1-2)

This joy in the law of God comes as we are increasingly drawn into the kingdom of God, finding in Christ and in the reign of Christ our true home.

But our hearts are inclined to other visions of the good life; we are not instinctively in alignment with the kingdom. Further, the kingdom is an acquired taste; for many it seems foreign, hardly life giving. We have all too easily come to assume that life is found in the cruise ship voyage where we are waited on hand and foot. We think that more wealth and more fame and more power will somehow mean more happiness. And we find satisfaction in that which cannot ultimately fulfill the longings of our souls—career success, prestige, and power.

Thus, to pray in Spirit is to pray that the Spirit would show us Jesus—that we would see Christ lifted up and be drawn into the life-giving orbit of the ascended Lord. To this end we respond eagerly to the prompting of the Spirit—the ways in which the Spirit is calling us and wooing us to come into greater alignment with the kingdom.

It is important to stress that there is indeed much that is wrong with our world. And a prayer of confession is not an acquiescence to that wrong—whether our own wrongdoing or that of others. It is an act of alignment—in our own hearts and minds—with the reign of Christ; it is a way of saying,

"Thy kingdom come, and may it begin with me." It is a conscious and deliberate longing that the kingdom of God would come. But more, it is an affirmation that even as we work for the good, the noble, and the just, we cannot presume that we are embodiments of this goodness. In the church and in the world, we will be advocates for the good. And we will denounce injustice. But we will not presume that we somehow have already arrived. We will humbly acknowledge that we too are pilgrims, seeking to find our way.

MAKING CONFESSION IN THE SPIRIT

Now, before we actually look at the mode and content of our confession, we need to stress two things. First, confession is not a matter of getting God to love us. Indeed, we make confession precisely because we know we are loved. This is why, in part, the sequence is important: from thanksgiving to confession to discernment. We come to confession knowing that we are loved, grateful for the diverse and remarkable ways God has been good to us.

Second, confession is not about restoring a relationship with God. Sometimes it is said that sin breaks our relationship with God and that in making confession we are "getting right with God." But it is more helpful to recognize that we are already in relationship with him. We are his daughters and sons; nothing has changed or can change that. It is similar to the way my son might do wrong and come to me to make it right—he comes precisely because he is my son.

Mesa County Libraries
Thank you for checking out the following items:

Checked Out Items 9/21/2020 13:41
XXXXXXXXX3321

Item Title	Due Date
090061211017	10/12/2020 00:00
Teach us to pray / Gordon T. Smith.	

Checked out from the Central Library
www.mesacountylibraries.org
970-243-4442

In other words, we make confession as those who are in relationship with God and confident of God's love.

As those who are loved and know we are loved, we make confession. And as with thanksgiving it is also essential here that we learn to pray in the Spirit. We very specifically ask the Spirit to guide us in our praying: *Where are you, oh Spirit of God, calling me to turn?* This is a prayer of response to the convicting ministry of the Spirit. It is quite easy for us to look at ourselves and see a whole host of aspects of our lives that are not good. But the genius of praying in the Spirit is that it is the Spirit who guides us and calls us and convicts us of sin. And we turn, we make confession, specifically where and how the Spirit is leading us to confess.

With a tender heart—open and willing—we attend to the Spirit, who draws to our attention our frenetic and impatient spirit, or the harsh or unkind word spoken to a child or a neighbor, or the ease with which we slipped into gossip, or the failure to be generous, or the neglect of the created order, or the lack of courage to act or speak because we feared consequences or discomfort. Or perhaps what comes to mind is that we have neglected to observe the sabbath.

Now, we need to recognize that nothing is gained by false guilt—that is, the guilt we feel because we have failed to live up to the expectations of others or our own personal ideals. Rather, the genius of confession is that we are open—radically so—to where and how the Spirit guides us to make confession; the Spirit is the leader of this process. We come to our prayers from the disposition of the psalmist, who writes in Psalm 139,

> O LORD, you have searched me and known me.
> You know when I sit down and when I rise up;
>   you discern my thoughts from far away.
> You search out my path and my lying down,
>   and are acquainted with all my ways.
> Even before a word is on my tongue,
>   O LORD, you know it completely.
> You hem me in, behind and before,
>   and lay your hand upon me.
> Such knowledge is too wonderful for me;
>   it is so high that I cannot attain it.
> Where can I go from your spirit? (Psalm 139:1-7)

And then the prayer fittingly concludes,

> Search me, O God, and know my heart;
>   test me and know my thoughts.
> See if there is any wicked way in me,
>   and lead me in the way everlasting.
>   (Psalm 139:23-24)

We lean into the Spirit and trust the Spirit. We let the Spirit be the choreographer of our spiritual journeys. Rather than the catalog of our sins that our critics are more than happy to enumerate, and rather than our self-critique, which for many of us can be unduly harsh, we lean into the gentle inner witness of the Spirit. We ask: *Where, oh Spirit of God, are you calling me to confess and to turn and to grow in faith, hope, and love?*

THE CONTENT OF OUR CONFESSION

For what do we make confession? When we attend to the Spirit and lean into where and what the Spirit might be drawing our attention to, what might guide us in our praying? We can think, for one, of the Ten Commandments. We can also take note of the Sermon on the Mount—the very context in which we are asked to pray "forgive us our sins." But the whole scope of the biblical witness is surely the backdrop to the witness of the Spirit. We engage the biblical witness— from Genesis to Revelation. In other words, there are fundamentals of Christian identity and behavior that apply to all cultures and contexts.

But it is also appropriate to ask, What are the signs or indicators of holiness for *our* time, in our generation? Could it be that for Christians in different cultures and social contexts, while the holiness of God is always the holiness of God, there are crucial markers of holiness for this culture and this time?

For Christians who live in a secular age and a globalized world, what are the markers of holiness? In what ways are we being called to be "saints"—living expressions, as God grants grace, of God's character and holiness? One possibility—and I suggest it as only one example of how we are called to be a holy people—is hospitality. For the ancient church, in a pluralistic and pre-Christendom context, hospitality was a key marker of Christian identity. And perhaps it should be for the contemporary Christian community as well.

Another possibility is a continued resolve to be a just people and a commitment to social justice—that as individual Christians and as a Christian community we would recognize that worship that is not matched by a commitment to the poor and the marginalized is false worship (see Isaiah 58).

Or perhaps the observance of sabbath will be another marker of holiness in our day. In a culture where consumerism is a god, sabbath observance might be as powerful a signal as anything that we are living in tune with another kingdom.

In all of this, morality matters, especially in regard to our speech, our finances, and how we live with integrity around matters of sexuality. Speech, finances, and sexuality: these three recurring themes or threads course their way through the book of Proverbs, the words of Jesus in the Sermon on the Mount, and the writings of the apostle Paul when he describes how Christians are different. These are the key indicators of moral intelligence. And so all three will emerge when we reflect on how we are aligned with the kingdom of God. Yet sin is not merely a matter of morality; it is first and most crucially about whether all that we are—our thinking, our affections, the pattern of our lives, and our morality—is in alignment with the fact that Christ sits on the throne of the universe. Thus we see the genius of the classic prayers of confession that speak of "thought, word, and deed, by what

I have done and by what I have failed to do." That covers the landscape; it encompasses the full breadth of our human experience. What we have thought, what we have said, what we have done. And, just as significant, what we have failed to do.

We also need to recognize the insidious power of fear. In a post-Christian, secular, and pluralistic society, the greatest threat to our Christian identity is internal, not external: it is fear. And thus it is imperative that we monitor our hearts and our fears and confess the sin of fear when we have gotten into the morass of living with anxiety, fretfulness, and worry—whenever we have allowed fear to inform our choices, everything from our financial decisions to our voting behavior. Fear is a sign that we have not recognized or fully come to live within the freedom of the kingdom of God.

Whether it is on matters of morality or fear or any other aspect of the Christian life, the essential thing is that we are making confession for ourselves. We are not making a judgment about or making confession for our spouses, our children, the other members of our church, or our colleagues where we work. We are not asking this for our society or culture. We are rather considering our own lives and asking, What would our lives look like if in this social, historical, and economic context we were truly seeking to live in light of the kingdom of God? We are not complaining about other people; we are reflecting on our own lives and asking what it means for us, with our understanding of the reign of Christ, to live faithful to the coming of the kingdom of God. We are making confession for ourselves.

MAKING CONFESSION

How then do we make confession? What does it mean to have penitential prayers?

First and fundamentally, we make confession out of a deep conviction that Christ has gone before us and is for us; thus the value of the classic element in Christian liturgy known as the Agnus Dei:

> O Lamb of God, that takest away the sins of the
> world,
> Have mercy upon us.
> O Lamb of God, that takest away the sins of the
> world,
> Have mercy upon us.
> O Lamb of God, that takest away the sins of the
> world,
> Grant us thy peace.

With this conviction as the backdrop—or better put, as the *gateway*—to the prayer of confession, it is helpful to see confession as having five movements. Yes, confession is a single act; it is of a whole. And yet as we learn to make confession, consider the sequence of five distinct actions or dispositions.

We acknowledge wrong. To confess is to acknowledge that there is a disconnect: we live in a moral universe, a world of good and evil, and in some form or another, evil has intersected our lives. In thought, word, or deed we have been participants in what we know to be wrong. We have done or said that which we know is inconsistent with our confession of faith. We have failed to do what we very simply know we should have done. We know that evil, in some form, has come into our hearts and lives. We see the disconnect between what we know is true and right and good and our behavior in something that the Spirit has brought to our attention. We turn from judging others or blaming others. And we look to ourselves and the way we have been party to that which is inconsistent with the reign of Christ and our confession that Jesus is Lord.

We accept responsibility. It is vital—imperative—that we recognize that the heart of confession is that we take responsibility for our lives and for our behavior.

To make confession is to recognize a particular propensity: there is an inclination within each of us toward excusing ourselves. Just as Adam was inclined to blame Eve (Genesis 3:12), and Eve followed suit in not taking responsibility for her behavior, in like manner we all too easily acknowledge sin and wrong but then find an excuse: we claim extenuating circumstances, or that however wrong our behavior, it was understandable given that we were under huge pressure or because we had had a rough day at the office.

We too often rationalize our fears; we self-justify rather than face up to what we know is not our best selves. But instead of blaming others, we must accept adult responsibility for who we now are being called to be.

We seek the mercy of God. Having acknowledged our wrong—the sin that so easily invades our lives—and accepted responsibility for who we are and what we have done, we come to the central and defining moment of all worship, and particularly the worship of the penitent: the plea for mercy. We cast ourselves on the mercy of God; we have nowhere else to turn. We cannot vindicate ourselves; we cannot justify ourselves. Our only hope is that we would be able to live under and in the mercy of God.

And thus the ancient liturgical rubric called the Kyrie Eleison is so fitting, so timely, so universally appropriate: *Kyrie* (Lord) *eleison* (have mercy).

> Lord, have mercy.
> Christ, have mercy.
> Lord, have mercy on us all.

What we long for is the freedom that comes with learning to live, as Charles Williams is said to have put it, "under the mercy."

The Kyrie Eleison reflects an intentionality: an intellectual and emotional journey of moving into a conscious awareness of the mercy of God, over and around us. This is why we might even choose to sing the Kyrie in the privacy of our own personal prayers. There are many potential tunes we could use. What singing the Kyrie does is slow us down; it moderates the pace of our hearts so that, as the Kyrie is sung, we do not pass by too quickly or miss the wonder of this as our true rest: the mercy of God.

We appropriate the forgiveness of God. One of the great dangers in the practice of confession is that we would seemingly make confession—acknowledge our sin—but then not actually move through and out of confession as women and men who know, to the depth and core of our beings, that we are forgiven. We ought to know that indeed mercy has invaded our hearts and liberated us from the troublesome burden of guilt. This is why we need to consider the conscious appropriation of the forgiveness of God. We are set free, yes, but we are only free as we actually receive—appropriate—the forgiveness of God. This too is an essential and deliberate dimension of confession: to not only seek the mercy of God but then to receive it, and then also to act on the knowledge that we are forgiven, to benchmark this forgiveness in our hearts.

The liturgies of traditional churches therefore include this as an element of the worship: with confession comes "the Assurance of Pardon" or an equivalent, in which those who have made confession are declared forgiven. Some church communions speak of absolution. Whatever the rubric, the issue at hand is much the same: we are reminded, in the wonderful words of 1 John 1:9, that "if we confess our sins, he who is faithful and just will forgive us our sins and cleanse us from all unrighteousness."

It is an article of Christian faith that the one who makes confession can live with a deep and palpable confidence in the forgiveness of God. This is our true home; we live under the mercy.

We turn and embrace the way of truth and light. Confession includes a conscious movement into the mercy and forgiveness of God. But it is important to stress that this forgiveness is not an end but a means to an end. Well, in one sense it is an end. This is our true home: we are forgiven. But with that confidence we then recognize that we are forgiven *so that* we will live lives of freedom in Christ, in greater alignment with the reign of Christ. We are forgiven not because God somehow tolerates sin but so that we will be freed from its oppressive power and grow in faith, hope, and love.

And so the very process of confession necessarily includes turning—the reorientation or realignment of our lives. We turn from gossip to speech that is consistent with our confession. We turn from anger to meekness. We turn from fear. Or, speaking more positively, we turn and resolve and then live in the new reality, the new way of being that is called forth through the prayer of confession.

Sometimes the adjustment may be very slight—a small course correction, one might say. But over time it can make all the difference in our lives, gradually altering the pattern of behavior that will shape our identity and way of being. Sailors know this: the slightest course correction at sea can have a profound impact over time.

As often as not, this is the way confession works: the change is not dramatic but incremental, not a revolution but rather a conscious realignment with the good, the noble, the excellent, and the true. Our speech is moderated, our spending habits are adjusted, our approach to hospitality takes a slightly new direction.

And yet change comes. Furthermore, change is welcomed. The prayer of confession becomes the pivot not only of our prayers but also of our spiritual journey. Those who grow and mature and flourish in their Christian journey recognize that confession is the prayer that leverages their capacity to appropriate the transforming grace of the Spirit.

OUR MUTUAL FORGIVENESS

Before concluding these reflections on confession, I must make another important observation. The Scriptures are clear on this: there is no experience of the forgiveness of God that is not tied to our forgiveness of one another. We are taught to pray, "Forgive us our debts, as we also have forgiven our debtors" (Matthew 6:12). The reconciliation we have with God is linked to our reconciliation with one another. And thus it behooves us to keep short accounts not only with God but also with our neighbors—colleagues, the people we live with, the family member we are estranged from. In other words, our personal practice of confession keeps us attentive to any kind of underlying conflict or unresolved wrong that, while it might not seem

to be festering, signals that in some form or another there is
something amiss in a relationship.

In some cases reconciliation is not possible. But with a commitment reflecting the instruction of Romans 12:18, we do all
we can so that, so far as it depends on us, we are at peace with
all. We take the lead, however awkward the step, toward peace,
reconciliation, and mutual forgiveness. We do our part; we
make the overture. If the other does not choose to respond in
peace, we grieve this, but we do so knowing that we have taken
the steps we can take to bring about reconciliation.

A question naturally arises when we speak of our mutual
forgiveness: Use the one conditional on the other? Does God
forgive us only when we forgive our neighbor? Perhaps the
best way to appreciate this is to see that there is, no doubt, a
profound connection between the two. But it is not so much
that our behavior toward others fulfills a condition for God's
forgiveness of us as that when we know the forgiveness of
God we will forgive others. And if we don't—if we refuse, if
we continue to carry the grudge—our hearts will not be able
to fully appreciate the goodness and mercy of God.

REPENTANCE AND THE SACRAMENTAL
LIFE OF THE CHURCH

Finally, it is important to understand the relation between
confession and the sacramental life of the church. First, it is
very helpful to think of confession as the practice by which we
renew our baptismal vows and choose, again, to live in a

manner—in thought, word, and deed—that is consistent with our confession—that is, consistent with our baptismal identity. Our baptism is *the* fundamental benchmark of our lives: it speaks to our identity, our union with Christ, our vow or commitment to live in light of the kingdom. And confession is the means by which we return to that vision for our lives.

And second, we need to consider the table of mercy—the Lord's Table—the meal of reconciliation. In my upbringing, the Lord's Supper was not a happy meal. We were urged to "examine" ourselves lest we participate in an unworthy manner. And we were warned that if we participated unworthily, we might bring judgment on ourselves and others.

But this perspective, unfortunately, failed to highlight the wonder that Christ Jesus, in real time, is hosting this meal. The Lord of mercy welcomes us. He made breakfast for Peter—the same Peter who had denied him three times (John 21). Even so, he hosts us at the table. As sinners in need of grace, as those who long to know the forgiveness of God, we come. And we experience the Lord's Supper as a table of mercy: as the very place we come when we recognize our sin and failure and long to know the forgiveness of God. We come to the table, again and again; it is the meal of reconciliation.

And it is this meal that anchors our prayers: our prayers of thanksgiving, in that this meal is a Eucharist; our prayers of confession, in that this is the table of mercy.

THE PRAYER OF DISCERNMENT

Let your work be manifest to your servants,
and your glorious power to their children.
Let the favor of the Lord our God be upon us,
and prosper for us the work of our hands—
O prosper the work of our hands!

PSALM 90:16-17

Unless the LORD builds the house,
those who build it labor in vain.
Unless the LORD guards the city,
the guard keeps watch in vain.
It is in vain that you rise up early
and go late to rest,
eating the bread of anxious toil;
for he gives sleep to his beloved.

PSALM 127:1-2

GOD'S WORK AND OUR WORK

Psalm 90 speaks of the work of God—verse 16, "let your work be manifest"—and our work—verse 17, "prosper the work of our hands." When we pray "thy kingdom come," we also come to discernment—seeking to recognize and confirm how we are called to participate in the kingdom purposes of God. And yet to understand prayer as discernment requires an appreciation of this unique counterpoint between our work and the work of God.

First, our prayers assume that God acts benevolently in response to our petitions. That, in the language of Psalm 127:1, it is the Lord who "builds the house." When we pray, we are asking God to act: we make an intercession in which our specific request is that God will intervene and make a difference in our world. We pray for God to do what God—and in many ways, only God—can do. We pray out of a deep conviction that not only is God good, but also God has the capacity to heal and restore.

But often one gets the sense from Christians that the work of God co-opts or somehow eliminates any significance to our work. Some actually speak of prayer in this way: that we need to pray more and work less, suggesting that if we truly believe in God and have faith in God, we will spend less time in our efforts and more time "on our knees."

Yet this does not seem to be the perspective of the Scriptures. To the contrary: the Bible routinely witnesses to the significance of human agency and actually highlights the work of human persons. Psalms 90 and 127 both testify to the importance of human effort. The prayer of Psalm 90 is that God would "prosper the work of our hands" (v. 17). And as we see from Psalm 127, precisely *because* the Lord is the builder, our building—our work—is not in vain. Our work matters; it makes a difference. Faith is evident in dependent prayer, of course. But it is also evident in how we embrace the work to which we are called, knowing that our work matters. We refuse to despair or throw up our hands, disillusioned that nothing we do actually makes a difference. Instead, we see in the Scriptures that our work has significance.

We see this with the witness of Proverbs 31:10-31, which celebrates the work of a wise woman. We recognize also that there was human agency in the liberation of the people of Israel in the exodus. Who brought the people out of Egypt? Was it God or was it Moses? Or was it actually both? In the book of Acts, is the story of the early church the account of the work of the Spirit? Or the work of the apostles? Of course, it is both. The incarnation of the Son of God involves an extraordinary counterpoint between the Spirit and a young woman of ancient Palestine. She is invited to be the God-bearer, to be the one through whom the Christ-child will come. And all history hangs in the balance while the angel Gabriel waits for her breathtaking response: "Here am I, the servant of the Lord; let it be with me according to your word" (Luke 1:38).

In other words, could it be that while the work of God is truly foundational, God invites our participation, and our involvement in what God is doing actually matters? Truly our work does make a difference. God is always the lead actor in the drama of God's redemptive purposes in the world. But we are invited to be involved: to bring our talents, capacities, and ambition to the stage as well. This is affirmed in Psalm 90, which very specifically asks of God that the work of our hands would be confirmed and established.

Can God act unilaterally in response to our prayers? Of course. Is the God we worship capable of intervening, in mercy and power, to bring about redemptive and lasting change in a way that bypasses human actions or endeavors? Without doubt.

But this is not God's usual mode of engagement with our world. Most commonly, God's salvation incorporates the contributions of those God invites to be participants in what most needs to be said and done. He uses surgeons to bring about healing; he calls business people to build the economic foundation of our society. God calls preachers to proclaim the Word and teachers to guide us into an understanding of the wonders of creation. God calls artists and civil servants. God calls managers and administrators to be his partners in the work of building institutions and providing effective governance for those organizations.

The crucial point is that our work is an act of *response to* and participation in the work of God. As the secondary actors, we take our cues from God—very specifically, from the Spirit of God—as we contribute, in word and deed, to the kingdom purposes of God.

We should recognize here that the common mantra "pray more, give more, serve more" is simply unhelpful. Perhaps worse than unhelpful. It feeds a certain temptation: we think we are more significant if we do *more* and that we bring greatest glory to God if we accomplish *more*.

But the genius of good work as human agents is that our work is done in response to the call of God. And we do no more and no less than that which we are called to do as those who pray "thy kingdom come." On the one hand, we accept our limits. We are free to sleep at night in peace, as noted in the wonderful witness of Psalm 127:2:

> It is in vain that you rise up early
>   and go late to rest,
> eating the bread of anxious toil;
>   for he gives sleep to his beloved.

We are not carrying the weight of the world on our shoulders.

But on the other hand, we also accept, with alacrity, the roles, responsibilities, and opportunities that *are* given to us. We respond with eagerness and courage where we are called to act, in word and deed. Thus, when it comes to our work, less might actually be more. We are called to do no more—no less, of course, but also no more—than what is required of us by God. We can do our work confident that God is the builder (Psalm 127:1). We are not called to more and more and more; we are not called to be heroes; we are only called to do what we are called to do. No more and no less.

In our homes, our church communities, and our places of work, we will have long days, no doubt—for the farmer in seedtime and harvest, for the teacher in the preparation of new courses before the beginning of a new academic year, for the preacher doing one last revision of her sermon before Sunday (hopefully not on Saturday night!), and for the accountant who has a whole set of clients needing help to file their taxes on time. But this is not the norm. There are rhythms to our work—times of engagement and times of rest. And we discern: What is the good work to which we are called? What is it, as we participate in the kingdom of God, that we are called to say and called to do?

Thus the need for discernment—the prayer by which and in which we attend to the inner witness of the Spirit, who guides, nudges, and prompts us toward the work to which we are being called.

Notice then that if we are overworked and frenetically busy, it is a sign that we are not praying well—not actually discerning. And if we are puttering about, lacking focus or clarity or courage to do what needs to be done, then again the problem is a lack of prayerful engagement—a lack of discernment.

DISCERNMENT IS COMPLICATED

Having stressed that discernment is essential—imperative if we are to speak and act well—we need to acknowledge that it is difficult. Discernment is a messy and complicated process.

It comes easily to no one. This is true for a couple of reasons, and both have to do with what we might call the noise or distraction factor. First, there are external noises, and second, no less distracting, there are internal noises.

When it comes to external noise it is helpful to recognize that the Spirit's presence in our lives is, as often as not, a quiet witness—the "sound of sheer silence," to use the language from Elijah's experience described in 1 Kings 19:11-13. And the challenge here is twofold. First, frequently our religious context assumes that God's speaking is dramatic and overt; we are typically so impressed with such experiences that we tend to discount the slow and quiet work of the Spirit. But second and more crucial is that we live in what is aptly called an age of distraction. Discernment is very difficult in a world of continual interruption, whether it be visual distractions or the short attention span fostered by our electronic devices. When the Spirit moves quietly in our hearts, we have a challenge: How do we attend to the Spirit when our minds are conditioned to respond to every beep of our cell phones? How do we listen to God when we have this huge inner pressure to check our email? How can we be truly responsive to the inner witness of the Spirit when we have spent hours in malls that are a continual barrage of visual overload? And how can we be aware of the Spirit's movement in our hearts when the advertising industry pummels us with constant reminders of all that we lack?

But then we also need to address the internal noise. Discernment is complicated, and we should be rightly cautious in our discernment because we know our own hearts. We need to face the reality that we cannot trust ourselves. We so easily want to justify ourselves; we so easily get caught in a pattern of doing all we can to prove ourselves to ourselves and to God, to vindicate ourselves. We live in a private inner world of doubt and insecurity.

And this is complicated by the sheer volume of things for which we might feel responsible: at home, at the office, in our church communities, and in the towns and cities in which we live. We come up against need every day—more need on any given day than we can possibly respond to meaningfully. We are trying to make decisions about so many different things at once.

Further, discernment is particularly challenging when we face difficult relationships—whether at home, at church, in our work situation, or in our social context. Discernment is rarely easy, but it is doubly challenging when we are experiencing significant criticism or when the behavior of others around us seems deeply misaligned with our convictions about what is right and wrong.

Often we are inclined to think that if something is clearly wrong—that is, if it runs against common sense or the testimony of Scripture or breaks an agreed-on contract—then discernment is not needed. The situation is wrong; the Bible says it is wrong. End of discussion. Why discern? We are inclined to think that our anger and frustration with the situation is entirely justified; ours is a holy anger, surely. And we must do everything we can to act on this frustration and anger and either oppose or protest what is happening.

Yet even in these kinds of circumstances discernment is required. Jesus went to the cross after Gethsemane, even though there is no doubt that the cross was a great wrong, a violation of justice.

Sometimes, such as when a pipeline is about to be built through our backyard, our prayers will lead us to action: we do all we can to block the construction of something that threatens our environment and fosters further dependence on fossil fuels. And sometimes when something happens with which we disagree—perhaps in a church context where we voted in the minority on an issue that is of utmost important to us—we are called to quietly accept the outcome and live graciously in harmony with those we differ with. Sure, some might discern that this situation means they now must leave this church. But often we come to a quiet acceptance and to graciously being present as a minority voice.

And yet, how is one to know? How can we know whether we are acting peremptorily or whether we are being compliant merely out of fear of conflict? How are we to avoid acting rashly on the one hand or being subdued into passive acquiescence on the other? The answer, of course, is discernment. We ask, *Lord, for this context and in this setting, how are you calling me to respond?* We plead, *Oh Spirit of Christ, what is asked of me and required of me in this context and in light of this development?* Yet the point remains: when we feel threatened or angry or dismayed with a situation, discernment is that much more complicated.

We live in a busy, complicated world; discernment is always a matter of doing the best we can with this complexity and noise. Thus we should not be impressed with those who speak with great ease of what the Spirit has told them and how the Spirit has guided them. The more confident a person is that God has spoken to them, the more inclined we need to be to doubt their capacity for discernment. When someone makes constant references to how the Lord led them to do this and to say that, we are right in wondering whether discernment has actually happened. In few areas of our lives is humility more appropriate than here. We all need a good dose of humility on this score—a humility that acknowledges the noise in our world, along with a healthy self-doubt.

But even with this caveat, discernment is possible. It can be done. We can learn—even if we see in a mirror, dimly (1 Corinthians 13:12)—to know the voice of Jesus and the witness of the Spirit. We are not hamstrung by the noise around us or within us. But any confidence we do have must be rooted in a good process of discernment. We cannot presume we already know the call of the Spirit; our only hope is to learn to pray with discernment.

LEARNING DISCERNMENT

Discernment is indeed learned. But first we must learn what it means to give thanks and learn how to make confession.

We come to the prayer of discernment with gratitude. Insofar as we are able to discern, it is only possible if we are a grateful people who live with an affective awareness of the love of God. Thus the sequence of our prayers matters: we begin with thanksgiving. We cannot discern what God is calling us to be and do if we are not grateful for what God has done already.

Further, we can discern well only if we learn to make confession. This is so in part because sin blinds us; it complicates the movement of our hearts. We can discern only where there is simplicity of intent and desire. Thus we need to make confession. Confession is also crucial for a second reason: all too easily we act, at home or in the workplace, out of a false pressure or guilt. And what confession does is free us—from guilt, no doubt, but also from *false* guilt. If we are to be able to discern what God is calling us to do in the face of so much that needs to be done and could be done, we need to come to our prayers of discernment with some measure of freedom. We need to be always attentive to the ways in which we may be trying to prove ourselves or vindicate ourselves or cover for our fears. Thus confession comes before discernment in the sequence of our prayers.

Then, in gratitude and from a penitential disposition, we seek to prayerfully discern: *For this day, what is the good work to which I am called? In what ways am I being invited to be a participant in what God is doing?* In freedom—the freedom that comes through thanksgiving and confession—we attend to the call of God.

When it comes to discernment, there are three central and defining principles that can guide us in our prayers. Actually, in the masterpiece of spiritual guidance *The Spiritual Exercises of St. Ignatius*, they are called "rules of discernment." What follows here is adapted from Ignatius's rules, which reflect the best wisdom of the church on what it means to practice discernment in our prayers.

The term *rules* may strike some readers as a bit presumptuous, with the thought that perhaps we should speak of *guidelines* or *suggestions* instead. But the language of *rules* captures precisely how we need to think about discernment. It is comparable, I would suggest, to the rules of flight. A flight instructor does not refer to the principles of aerodynamics as "suggestions." Rather, there are *rules* of flight: this is how it works for a heavier-than-air vehicle to actually take to the skies. In like manner, the rules of discernment are quite simply how the Spirit works in our lives and in our prayers. These rules reflect the wisdom of the church across the generations, testified to not only by Ignatius but also in diverse ways and forms by each of the spiritual masters in the history of the church.

It is helpful to think of the rules as three defining principles that guide effective discernment—essential ways in which we think about the guidance of the Spirit in our prayers.

First, it is a basic principle of discernment that in our prayers we are seeking the *best*. People often think that discernment is a matter of good or evil: we discern what is good and then reject what is not good. There is some truth in this, of course, but for the maturing Christian it is not so simple. Ignatius suggests that for sincere and committed Christians, the genius of temptation is that we are tempted not with evil but with the lesser good. We are distracted from the good to which we are called by something that is good in itself but is not the good to which we have been called; it is a "good" that we have chosen for, perhaps, all the wrong reasons. It is the lesser good.

When we discern, we are very specific in asking, *What is the good to which I am called?* We recognize that the evil one is quite content to distract us by seeing that we are engaged in that which, while not evil in itself, is not the good that God is inviting us to embrace. The good, then, is the enemy of the best. Thus wise Christians know that we can fill our days with good things—good deeds, even—and in the process actually neglect the good to which we are called. No matter how good the "good" is, it is still not obedience to the call of God if it is not the good to which I am called—or better put, if I am neglecting the good that reflects the call and purposes of God in my life. Discernment is about attending to the particular good that reflects the call of God on our lives.

Some find it helpful to actually put the choice down on a piece of paper—to write out the options and possibilities, however limited these might be in some cases, and then ask why one option over the other might be best.

Second, as a basic principle of discernment, it is imperative that we recognize and affirm that the Spirit guides in peace and that the inner witness of the Spirit leads to joy. The ancient word for this orientation of the heart is *consolation*. The counter of consolation is *desolation*. The rule of discernment is clear: we choose in consolation; we do not trust desolation. We do not choose in desolation: we do not act when our hearts are inclined toward anger, discouragement, fear, or any sense of spiritual malaise. We do not choose in anger; we do not act out of discouragement; we refuse to make a critical life choice if fear is potentially informing our decision making. The Spirit leads in peace, and thus discernment means that we act only in peace.

And third, as critical as anything, the peace must be tested. We do not assume that if we are in consolation, this consolation necessarily comes from God. Even if we have good feelings about something—peace that something seems right—discernment requires that we test and confirm that this peace genuinely comes from the Spirit.

This is typically the great error when it comes to prayer and discernment: the lack of actual discernment. People feel a great movement of the heart and fail to appreciate that deep sentimentality means nothing in its own right; it has meaning only if it is tested and if we can confirm that what we are feeling is genuinely of God. We should insist that however powerfully we believe that God has spoken to us, wise counsel keeps us cautious and hesitant. We remember the significance of Paul's bold declaration that "even Satan disguises himself as an angel of light" (2 Corinthians 11:14).

Indeed, the more confident a person is that they know what God has said and is saying, the more tentative we should urge them to be. There is nothing lost in acknowledging that we see in a mirror dimly. We can and must acknowledge our capacity for self-deception and for actually misreading the witness of the Spirit. We must move humbly and cautiously. That is, we must learn to discern. If we have thoroughly applied all the rules of discernment, we can move confidently forward—yet with an appropriate humility. And this means that we actually say the words "as best as I can tell," not out of a lack of confidence and not as pseudo humility, but as an acknowledgment of our human limitations.

But we can move confidently—we can speak and act with grace and courage—if we have applied the basic principles of discernment to our prayers. This means that we need to learn to test the peace so that as much as possible we can say that indeed we are speaking and acting in a way that aligns with the kingdom purposes of God in our world and in our lives.

TESTING THE PEACE: THREE QUESTIONS

To be clear: we can only discern if we are attentive to what is happening to us emotionally. The context or setting for the Spirit's guidance in our lives will be the movement of our hearts. And thus we need to learn to trust our hearts and lean into the peace that resides there. But we can trust our hearts only if there is a genuine and extensive approach to testing and proving whether the tenor of our hearts does truly reflect the presence and fruit of the Spirit in our lives. We can trust our hearts only if we have tested—discerned—that what is happening within us is truly of God.

It is helpful to test the peace by asking three questions of our experience of peace. First, does this peace reflect the will and purposes of God as revealed in Scripture? This test is crucial; the inner witness of the Spirit will always be consistent with the *inscripturated* witness. There will always be a deep congruity between the testimony of the Old and New Testaments and the purposes of the Spirit in our prayers and in our lives. This does not mean there is a one-to-one correlation between the two. The counterpoint of Word and Spirit does not mean that we actually do not need the Spirit because we have the Bible. Some conclude that we can just read the Bible and know what to do, what decisions to make, and what course of action is appropriate. But the genius of the task of discernment is that the ancient Word is made present by the Spirit; we are essentially asking, How is the Spirit inviting us to live *now*, in light of the ancient biblical witness? Thus, as women and men immersed in the Scriptures, we can and must attend to the Spirit and ask how the Spirit is guiding us. And there will be a deep congruity between the witness of the Scriptures and our experience of the Holy Spirit.

Second, the witness of the Spirit also needs to be tested by the examination of our inner orientation and motive. We can ask, What is the driving and defining motivation that shapes my desires through this discernment process? We seek to know the grace of "holy indifference"—that is, freedom from misguided or inordinate desires. We turn from the craving for financial security, or for honor and affirmation, or for power and influence. Yes, we do have legitimate needs for basic financial stability and affirmation and the potential for influence. But these needs so easily distract us and co-opt our capacity to long for nothing other than the glory of God and the freedom to be all that God is calling us to be. And so we ask for this freedom—the freedom to simply say, "your will be done."

And third, we need to ask in the process of discernment, To whom am I legitimately accountable for the actions or choices I make? Here is a simple rule of thumb: we cannot discern well if we are not in community. More specifically, it has to be community where there is very genuine accountability—that is, the capacity of others to either confirm or challenge what it is that we think God is saying to us. We are so easily misguided and so easily inclined to justify ourselves and our actions. Thus we must test, with others—faithful companions on the way—whether what we are sensing is truly from God.

Without doubt there will be those who differ with us; discernment is also about the courage to do what we need to do, even if there are voices that disagree. Perhaps they will differ very strongly. But that is never an excuse for not consulting others and being accountable to others. Rather, in humility, even when there are those who differ with us, we live with a deep accountability to those who legitimately have a voice, a perspective relevant to our decisions—those who can confirm with us that we have discerned well or, as the case may be, gently suggest that we do not have a good read on what the Spirit is saying. Not all who oppose or differ with us are a legitimate source of accountability. As a university president, I report to a board; a pastor reports to a council of elders; a faculty member is accountable to a dean; a husband is accountable to his wife. These are all essential expressions of accountability. We will have those who differ with us, but not all have the right to challenge us.

So there are three questions by which we test the peace:

- Is there a congruency with the testimony of the Scriptures?

- Is my heart orientation one of holy indifference?

- Is there affirmation from those I am legitimately accountable to?

What we find through this discernment process is that, just as with thanksgiving and confession, we grow in humility—a meekness of heart. And it is this very humility that then, in turn, provides us with the courage to say what we are being called to say—not with anger or frustration, but with words spoken even in conflicted and potentially stressful situations with grace and peace. And we have the courage to do what we are being called to do. We have tested the peace. We now act. Yes, of course, petition is still very much part of our prayers. We ask God to do what only God can do in our circumstances and in our world. But we have also discerned, through *our* speaking and acting, the ways that God is inviting us to participate in what God is doing.

DISCERNMENT AND THE LORD'S SUPPER

The Lord's Supper is the holy Eucharist; it embodies our thanksgiving before God. It is the table of mercy; here we come to and are reanimated by the forgiveness of God and once more aligned with the reign of Christ in our lives and in our world.

And then also, the Lord's Table is critical to the prayer of discernment. At this meal our hope is renewed, for this is the feast that anticipates the great feast at the triumph of the reign of Christ. This meal also fosters clarity about our ultimate allegiance and loyalty—to the living and ascended Christ. We see, for example, the exquisite encounter between Jesus and Peter described in John 21, where at breakfast—and the meal is not incidental—Jesus three times asks Peter if Peter loves him and then confirms his call on Peter's life. Further, the Lord's Supper is a holy meal; it is food for the road, "the gifts of God for the people of God," to strengthen our wobbly legs and our feeble hearts. The prayer of discernment will consistently bring us to the point of needing to say what needs to be said and do what needs to be done. But so easily our fears impede our way. And so we come to the table—the Eucharist, the table of mercy—and we find hope, greater clarity, and renewed strength. Our eyes are lifted up; our hearts and minds are strengthened. In the words of the Book of Common Prayer, we are invited to the table with the call "feed on him in your hearts by faith."

Again, prayer is embodied. In this case, the prayer of discernment also brings us to the Lord's Table so that we not only attend to the Spirit but are then empowered by the Spirit to be and do what the Spirit is calling us to be and do.

PRAYER AS SPIRITUAL PRACTICE

*t*hrough prayer we come into greater alignment with the reign of Christ in our lives and in our world. We become women and men of the kingdom. But this does not happen in one swoosh—one dramatic prayer or even a transformative prayer retreat. It comes slowly and gradually—yes, through prayer, but prayer as the pattern and rhythm of our days. This is prayer as habit, as a spiritual practice: prayer that is integrated into the way in which we spend our time and our days, as something that we do again and again and again. We learn to judge or evaluate our prayers not by whether we experience something immediate or dramatic, but by whether over time we grow into greater appreciation for the meaning, purpose, and life of the kingdom.

The reign of Christ—the kingdom—orders our lives as we pray. And yet this ordering of our lives happens slowly and incrementally. The kingdom of God becomes our compass and our lens—that is, our direction, but also the way by which we see our lives and our world—as we learn to pray and as we learn to do it regularly, consistently, and persistently. We long for our lives to be caught up in the kingdom, to seek the kingdom more than anything else (Matthew 6:33). And this requires persistent prayers—ideally daily—for the very simple reason that the impact of our prayers is their cumulative effect. We make our prayers again and again, judging their effectiveness by their fruit over weeks, months, and even years of consistent practice. In time, the kingdom becomes second nature to us. It is our way of being, of seeing and responding to our world and the circumstances that we face—the good, the bad, the encouraging, and the challenging.

Gradually, as we attend to our prayers—habitually and consistently—we have greater clarity: we see ourselves and our world more clearly. Our behavior becomes more disciplined and focused; the virtues of faith, hope, and love are formed within us. Most of all, we are drawn into the life that is ours in Christ—bringing delight and glory to the Father as through the Spirit we find our deepest joy in Christ and in his kingdom. But the point is that this comes slowly and incrementally; it emerges in our lives through sustained practice over an extended period of time.

Nothing so indicates that the kingdom matters to us as the consistency of our prayers. It is not what we say about the kingdom, but rather that we seek it daily. We pray "thy kingdom come"—with thanksgiving, confession, and discernment—as a pattern and rhythm of our lives, and as we do it again and again and again, it matters to us more and more. We come to love the kingdom and the one who reigns on the throne of the universe.

LEARNING PRAYER WITH THE PSALMS

Once more, if we are to learn how to pray, we must—there is no other way—learn the Psalter and learn to pray with the Psalms. Prayer as spiritual practice begins and ends with the Psalms: praying the Psalms routinely and consistently, as the pattern not only of Sunday worship but also of our own personal prayers. These were the prayers of Jesus and of the apostles and the early church. We neglect them to our peril, in that they provide the antidote to worship forms and styles that infantilize the church with false comfort, forced sentimentality, and pseudo piety. The Psalms are the supreme means by which our hearts and minds are aligned, in our prayers, with the heart and mind of Christ. We pray "thy kingdom come" by praying the Psalms.

This is why there is much wisdom in praying the Psalms—perhaps a Psalm each day—in one's personal prayers. And this is why all ancient liturgies of the church were saturated with Psalms and included, at the very least, one Psalm as a vital element in each gathering for worship. This suggests to me that when we are in worship with a congregation and not one Psalm is included—either read, said, or sung—something is missing. For those in more "free"—for lack of a better word—forms of worship, worship that some think of as "nonliturgical" (though there is a sense in which all worship is by definition liturgical), I suggest that the people who are designing and leading worship consider the following. First, the Psalms are fundamental, and at the very least one Psalm—not merely a line here or there, but the Psalm as a whole—should be included in the order of worship. And second, in using the Psalms, we are praying, but we are also teaching the practice of prayer. Those who lead in worship are, of course, leading the congregation in worship, but they are also cultivating the practice of prayer that will inform the individual, personal prayers of those who are part of the shared liturgy of the church. And what better resource to do this with than the Psalms? What is better than coming back to the rhythm and focus of the Psalms in our shared liturgies so that the Psalms then inform our personal prayers?

In your daily prayers, perhaps start with a Psalm each day as you begin praying. Over three months you would then pray through all 150 Psalms, perhaps saving Psalm 119 for a weekend or praying it over two days in a month that has thirty-one days. Monastic communities have a daily routine and rhythm of prayer that gives them a way to pray the entire Psalter every month. And some Christians have formed urban communities to follow a similar order to their days, meeting at set points each day and very intentionally praying the Psalms in the heart of the city. But for most Christians, it is sufficient to attend to a Psalm a day.

Consider expanding to three a day during Lent through Easter Sunday so that over this season in the church calendar you pray through each of the Psalms. Pray a Psalm in the early morning, at noon, and in the evening, reflecting the words of Psalm 55:17, which speaks of evening, morning, and noon in what seemed to be a cycle of prayer beginning where the ancient Hebrew day began, at sundown.

Carry a copy of the Psalms in your briefcase or purse; have it at the ready on the commuting train to work, after you board a flight, or for a brief spring day respite on a park bench. Get to know the Psalms; make them your friends. And allow them to be the means by which the Holy Spirit draws you into thanksgiving, confession, and greater discernment.

PRAYER AND THE LIFE OF THE CHURCH

Even when we pray as individuals—our solitary and personal prayers—we rightly pray as those who are in fellowship with the church. And it only makes sense to be intentional about how our personal prayers reflect our life in community. In particular, our personal prayers should reflect our participation in the Sunday liturgy but also be a dynamic counterpoint to our Sunday worship and prayer. Then there will be an iterative quality to the connection, the counterpoint, with personal prayers drawing on the strength and shared experience of common prayer, and our experience of life in the Sunday liturgy informed by our personal prayers.

In this regard, I think in particular of four elements to the life of the church, or more specifically, the worship or liturgy of the church: the hymns of the faith, the ministry of the Word, the Lord's Supper, and the church calendar.

The hymns of the faith. In our shared worship, there are sung prayers of the people of God—"psalms, hymns, and spiritual songs," to use the language of Colossians 3:16. Ideally, we are actually singing psalms (Old Testament Psalms put to contemporary tunes), hymns (both ancient and contemporary), and songs (again, both older and newer melodies) that enable us to praise God in the company of sisters and brothers. We give thanks together and bind our hearts together in song. When our faith is weak, we sing knowing that strong voices—the voices of those whose faith is stronger on this day—will carry us along. And those same hymns can come back to us in our prayers during the week.

The ministry of the Word. The church devotes itself to "the apostles' teaching and fellowship" (Acts 2:42). And thus in community we attend—together—to the reading of Scripture, ideally with readings from both Old and New Testaments and specifically from the Gospels, and then we move with God's people to an attentiveness to the Word preached. And here we ask—again, in the company of sisters and brothers—for what it is that God is saying to us in Christ. We come to the text asking for illumination—that the Spirit would guide our hearing and equip us through the Word to be the people that we are called to be. And then through the week we can let this Word come back to us in our personal prayers, asking the Spirit that indeed the Word preached on Sunday will dwell within us (Colossians 3:16). We consciously choose to let the sermon that has been preached be something that has a continued place in our hearts and minds through the week following Sunday worship.

The Lord's Supper. Even as the church is devoted to "the apostles' teaching and fellowship," it is also devoted to "the breaking of bread and the prayers" (Acts 2:42). With God's people, we come to the celebration of the Eucharist and give thanks. We come to the table of mercy and renew the conscious awareness that we are forgiven. We come to the table of hope and nourishment and find renewed courage to be who we are called to be. Our personal prayers offered in solitude are anchored by and echoed in this meal shared in community.

The church calendar. Ideally, all of this happens within a church community that observes the church calendar: Advent, Christmas, Epiphany, Lent, Palm Sunday, Good Friday, Easter, Ascension, and Pentecost, and on to the grand conclusion to the church calendar, Christ the King Sunday. When our personal prayers are aligned with the church calendar, this too fosters our capacity to pray as those who, even when we are praying alone, are praying with the church. Through Advent, we begin with "O Come, O Come, Emmanuel"; we start slowly, feeling the pang of a world that is yet so deeply fragmented. And we move to the glory of

Christmas slowly and methodically. And then on to Epiphany. And then through Lent we slow down and accommodate our own spiritual practices, including our prayers, to the penitential season. And then into Holy Week, to Good Friday and Holy Saturday, and then of course Easter Sunday. Then our prayers take us toward Ascension Day and, fifty days from Easter, the feast of Pentecost, where in our prayers we appropriate afresh the grace and gift of the Holy Spirit in our lives. In praying with the church calendar, we choose to let the Christ story shape not only our shared worship and common life in the church but also our personal experience of thanksgiving, confession, and discernment.

THE PLACE AND FORM OF OUR DAILY PRAYERS

Place matters. Yes, of course, we can pray anywhere—on the bus, in traffic on the way to work, at the coffee shop, and in the kitchen as we or others are busy with preparations for meals. And yet good practice suggests that we learn to find a quiet space with minimal distractions—perhaps a solitary corner of the house, or a church on the route to your office that has doors open early to accommodate those who need a quiet place in the heart of the city. We are embodied souls; as such, the routines and rhythms of our prayers require some consideration for our need for quiet, solitary spaces to allow us to be able to give our full hearts and minds to our thanksgiving, our confession, and our discernment.

We also need to consider the actual form or structure of our personal prayers. There is no doubt that many struggle with the early morning. Their rhythms of sleep and rest and the cycles of their bodies seemingly war against doing anything that requires mental alertness any time before mid-morning! And yet, we do need to make a case for beginning our day— perhaps with an appropriate beverage in hand—with our prayers. It is so often the case for so many Christians that if they do not begin the day with prayer, it just never happens. A mother of school-age children might protest and rightly insist that the best time for prayer is immediately after the rest of the family have banged their way out of the house and off to school and work and she has the place to herself for a second cup of coffee and the space to give time to morning prayers. And no doubt there are other exceptions. But as a rule, for most of us the best time for daily prayer is first thing.

Find a quiet spot, with relatively few distractions or inter- ruptions, a space that can be your space if only for a few minutes: a sanctuary, a sacred space for your prayers. Set aside twenty minutes, perhaps thirty. It does not need to be longer. For those whose life and work takes them into the world or those who, like the mother just mentioned, are managing a home with growing children, thirty minutes is good and more than adequate to sustain a vital and engaging life of prayer.

Begin with a Psalm—perhaps as part of a plan to read and pray through the Psalms every three months.

Then move to thanksgiving. Ask of the Spirit, *For what should I be giving thanks today?* And take what comes to mind as of God—as gift, as the Spirit's calling to your attention the diverse ways in which God has been present to you. Think back over the previous day and see the many ways in which you have known the goodness of God. In times of darkness or significant discouragement, lean into the Spirit and ask for those essential signals of God's presence in your life.

Then make confession. Here too, think back over the last day and consider what the Spirit might bring to your attention. Perhaps it is something grievous, but as often as not the sin we need to confess is not some horrific thing we have done, some deep violation of conscience. Rather, often when we pray, "Search me, O God," what comes to mind is a word spoken harshly to a spouse, child, or colleague. Or perhaps a growing fear that needs to be named and acknowledged—something just under the surface that we need to bring into the open. Or perhaps it is the neglect of sabbath—not some deep violation, but simply that we were not fully as present to our sabbath as we should have been or could have been. For maturing Christians it is not so much the deep wrong as the seemingly minor points that if left unchecked eventually take us far astray. Again, like the ship that is off course by one degree, it is only a matter of time before we are way off. The Spirit draws to our attention those areas of our lives where a small course correction can and will ultimately make all the difference in our lives: in our relationships, in the pattern of our work, in the orientation of our hearts.

And then move to discernment. In our daily prayers, the focus will likely be a consideration of the day that is before us. To whom are you being asked to speak, and what words are you to offer? What are you being called to do—what priorities, what that is important and essential to your vocation (meaning that you do not merely attend to what seems urgent)? Where, for this day, will you need courage to speak and courage to act? And also, perhaps having discerned that we are called to wait and not act, we discern where we need to have the patience for this day to let God do God's work in God's time.

If you are facing a major life decision, a decision that will alter the contours of your life—marriage or a job transition, for example—the clarity about the call of God might not come right away. And so you can come back to this matter each day as part of your prayers. Or, alternatively, consider finding and setting aside a more extended time, perhaps a day of prayer.

With the opening Psalm, we can also consider a text of Scripture—from the sermon or the Scripture readings used in worship last Sunday, or our own readings as we meditate our way through Scripture. Many find it helpful to go from thanksgiving to confession and then to a text of Scripture before moving to a time of discerning prayer.

A LIFELONG JOURNEY

"Lord, teach us to pray." It is the longing of our hearts as new Christians; we know this matters. But we make this request through the whole of our lives—through midlife and into our senior years. We are always, one might say, learning to pray. We often come back to the basics of thanksgiving, confession, and discernment. But we also come to a deepened and growing appreciation of the nuances of our prayers and how, most of all, our prayers bring us into fellowship with Christ, the very one to whom we pray "thy kingdom come."

Transitions in our lives—through marriage, perhaps, or children, or changes in our family situation, or job changes— consistently will alter the routines and rhythms of our lives. And during such changes it is good to go back to the basics of prayer—to recognize that through each transition or new life situation, prayer remains as a basic spiritual practice. A practice that we are always learning and that always remains as a fundamental feature of our lives.

AFTERWORD

Prayer as Petition

*Do not worry about anything, but in everything
by prayer and supplication with thanksgiving
let your requests be made known to God.*

PHILIPPIANS 4:6

*P*etition will be an essential dimension of our prayers. For some, it will be an integral part of their daily prayers: they will move from thanksgiving to confession, to discernment, and then to prayers of petition. Alternatively, others will move on from their daily prayers with those things in mind that will inform their prayers through the day, and they will come back throughout the day to those points of petition that are on their hearts and minds.

Prayer is an act of service. We serve our neighbor and our world by interceding for the needs of the other. In some respects is it the most fundamental act of service that we can offer: to serve one another by praying for one another.

In prayers of petition, you can remember the following:

1. The needs of those who are closest to you—family and friends. You might pray as Paul did for Timothy: "I remember you constantly in my prayers night and day" (2 Timothy 1:3).

2. The place where you work, including the needs of your colleagues. Perhaps pray along the lines of the elder who penned 3 John, opening his letter to his colleague and companion Gaius with these words: "Beloved, I pray that all may go well with you and that you may be in good health, just as it is well with your soul" (3 John 2).

3. Your faith community—the church of which you are a part. Perhaps use as a guide the prayer of the apostle for the Ephesian church:

For this reason I bow my knees before the Father, from whom every family in heaven and on earth takes its name. I pray that, according to the riches of his glory, he may grant that you may be strengthened in your inner being with power through his Spirit, and that Christ may dwell in your hearts through faith, as you are being rooted and grounded in love. (Ephesians 3:14-17)

4. What is happening on the local, national, and global scene that merits your attention, beginning with your own neighborhood and city. Follow the call of Jeremiah 29:7, which reads, "But seek the welfare of the city where I have sent you into exile, and pray to the LORD on its behalf, for in its welfare you will find your welfare." This includes prayer for all those in civic authority (1 Timothy 2:1-2).

And then also in our prayers we can, of course, remember our own needs. Without apology we can ask for God's gracious mercy to be extended to us—our health and physical needs, the well-being of our work situation, the challenges we personally are facing—as we ask for wisdom, courage, and strength for the day.

When it comes to prayers of petition, we are wise to remember two points. First, these prayers do not have to be long; nothing is gained by length and wordiness. God is not impressed by many words and does not need new information. In our intercessions, we pray to the God who knows the situation for which we pray even better than we do (Matthew 6:7-8). Second, while it is not inappropriate to let other people know that we are keeping them in mind, as a rule, most of the prayers we offer should be offered in secret (Matthew 6:6). For each of these areas of petitionary prayer, we can pray, *Oh Spirit of God, guide me in my prayers—for what should I be praying as I pray for this person or this situation?*

Our prayers of petition and intercession assume that there are things that reflect our utter and absolute dependence on God—wherein we ask God to do what only God can do, and wherein we know that our only hope is that God would act. These prayers are never an "out" or a justification for our inaction. They are rather the deep longings and hopes of the world, the church, and our own hearts and minds—our pleas that God would act, that God would be present, that the grace of God would invade our world.

And the evidence that we are indeed women and men of prayer is that we do not worry about anything, but having made our requests known to God, we receive and know the peace that "surpasses all understanding" (Philippians 4:6-7).

Again, to stress: we pray prayers of petition as grateful people, as women and men who regularly make confession, and as those who are ever attentive, eagerly discerning where we are being called to speak and how we are being called to act. Petition assumes thanksgiving, confession, and discernment. But more, petition is really, in the end, nothing other than praying "thy kingdom come" in the lives of those we love, "thy kingdom come" within our church communities, and "thy kingdom come" within the cities where we live, the countries we call home, and the world that so deeply needs to know the saving power of the reign of Christ. This is our prayer.

NOTES

1 PRAYER AND THE KINGDOM OF GOD

8   *participate in heaven's invasion*: Darrell Johnson, *Fifty-Seven Words That Change the World: A Journey Through the Lord's Prayer* (Vancouver: Regent College Publishing, 2005), 19.

2 PRAYING IN THE SPIRIT

20   *a secular age*: This phrase has been coined by Canadian Roman Catholic scholar Charles Taylor in his defining publication, *A Secular Age* (Cambridge, MA: Harvard University Press, 2007).

3 THE PRAYER OF THANKSGIVING

38   *Ignatius Loyola, in his classic guide to prayer*: Ignatius Loyola, *The Spiritual Exercises of St. Ignatius*, trans. and ed. Louis J. Puhl (Chicago: Loyola University Press, 1975), #232-37.

42   *In this remarkable essay*: Dietrich Bonhoeffer, *Life Together and Prayerbook of the Bible*, trans. Daniel W. Bloesch and James H. Burtness (Minneapolis: Fortress, 1996), 36.

5 THE PRAYER OF DISCERNMENT

83   *rules of discernment*: Ignatius Loyola, *The Spiritual Exercises of St. Ignatius*, trans. and ed. Louis J. Puhl (Chicago: Loyola University Press, 1975), #313-36.

BOOKS BY GORDON T. SMITH

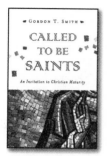

Called to Be Saints

Courage & Calling

Consider Your Calling

Listening to God in Times of Choice

Spiritual Direction

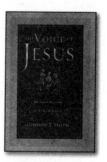

The Voice of Jesus

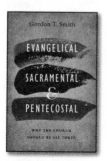

Evangelical, Sacramental & Pentecostal

Institutional Intelligence